*to Alan
Clearly man -
Pete.*

Literary Drinkers

By
Pete Bunten

Graphics & Design by Roger Buck

Literary Drinkers
Pete Bunten

Graphics & Design: Roger Buck

Published by
Pynot Publishing
56 Main Road
Holmesfield
Dronfield
Derbyshire
S18 7WT
England

Tel & Fax: 0114 289 0348
Email: info@pynotpublishing.co.uk

Find us on the World Wide Web at www.pynotpublishing.co.uk

First Published 2006

Copyright 2006 © by Pete Bunten.

Rights
All rights reserved. No part of this book may be reproduced or transmitted in any form or by any means, electronic or mechanical, including photocopying, recording, or by any information storage or retrieval system, without prior written consent from the publisher or author.

Printed and bound in the United Kingdom by JB Printing, Sheffield.

ISBN 0-9552251-0-8
ISBN 978-0-9552251-0-9

INTRODUCTION

Ernest Hemingway famously asserted that good writers were drinking writers, presumably including himself in both categories. Common sense, however, suggests that much great writing has been produced despite rather than because of the writer's drinking habit.
Many of the authors explored in this collection would also, quite rightly, bridle at the suggestion that they were themselves heavy or destructive drinkers. English Literature is nevertheless the richer for the wide range of talented writers who have turned their pen or word processor to the world of drinking and - in the British Isles especially - beer drinking. Hence the excuse for this series.
If beer, or ale, or porter floats and froths at the heart of a culture it would be surprising if it did not also help to define that culture through the works of its greatest writers.
This ubiquity brings its own hazards, however. I am aware of the limited range of the writers here on offer. The Americans are barely mentioned, despite their writers' well-attested drinking lives. There are no women writers listed here. The only weak excuses that can be offered are the wealth and breadth of available material and the desperate attempt to keep the focus on beer, and good beer at that. Perhaps that suggests possibilities for a future edition. Let us hope so. It might provide a necessary motive for you, the reader, to ensure this edition sells out.

The author and illustrator would like to record their appreciation of the support of the Chesterfield & District Branch of CAMRA in whose magazine, 'Innspire', these articles originally appeared, and in particular the advice and hard work of Nick Wheat without whom this edition might not have been possible. The author would also like to record his thanks to Lorna Morris, most loyal and discriminating of readers, and to his supportive and tolerant daughters, Catherine and Anna.

BIBLIOGRAPHY

The author would like to record his references and debt to the following publications:

Kingsley Amis: 'I Like it Here', Penguin 1968 (Victor Gollancz). 'Lucky Jim', Penguin, 1970. 'The Old Devils', Hutchinson, 1986. 'The Letters of Kingsley Amis' ed. Z. Leader, Harper Collins, 2000. Samuel Beckett: 'Collected Shorter Plays of Samuel Beckett' Faber, 1984. 'Waiting for Godot' Faber, 1968. James Knowlson: 'Damned to Fame. The Life of Samuel Beckett'Bloomsbury,1996. Brendan Behan: 'Brendan Behan's Island' Hutchinson 1962. 'Hold Your Hour and Have Another', Hutchinson, 1963. 'Brendan Behan's New York', Hutchinson, 1984. 'The Quare Fellow', Methuen, 1965 Hilaire Belloc: 'The Complete Verse of Hilaire Belloc', Pimlico 1991 (Peters, Frazer &. Dunlop). Jeffery Bernard: 'Low Life', Duckworth 1993. 'Reach for the Ground', Duckworth 1996. Charles Bukowski: 'The Movie, Barfly', Black Sparrow Press, 1995. 'Hot Water Music', Black Sparrow Press, 1983. Robbie Burns: 'Poems and Songs of Robert Burns' ed James Barke, Collins 1966. Catherine Carswell: 'The Life of Robert Burns', Canongate, 1990. Geoffrey Chaucer: 'The Works of Geoffrey Chaucer', ed. F.N. Robinson, OUP, 1968. G.K.Chesterton: 'The Collected Poems of G.K.Chesterton', Methuen (A P Watt Ltd). John Clare: 'Selected Poems', Penguin, 2000. 'The Parish', Penguin, 1986. Jonathan Bate: 'John Clare. A Biography', Picador, 2003. Charles Dickens: 'Selected Journalism, 1850-1870', Penguin, 1997. 'A Tale of two Cities', Penguin, 1986. 'Barnaby Rudge', Penguin Classics, 2003. 'The Old Curiosity Shop', Penguin, 1983. 'The Pickwick Papers', Penguin, 1977. Kenneth Grahame: 'The Wind in the Willows', Methuen, 1940. 'Paths to the River Bank', Souvenir Press, 1983. Patrick Hamilton: 'Hangover Square', Penguin,1974. 'Twenty Thousand Streets Under the Sky', The Hogarth Press, 1987. Thomas Hardy: 'Jude the Obscure', Macmillan, 1974. 'Chosen Poems of Thomas Hardy', Macmillan, 1975. 'Far from the Madding Crowd', Macmillan, 1965. 'The Trumpet Major', Penguin,1997. 'Tess of the D'Urbervilles', Penguin, 1985. 'Oxford Readers' Companion to Hardy', Oxford, 2000. Jaroslav Hasek: 'The Good Soldier Svejk', Penguin, 1981. Bohumil Hrabal: 'I Served the King of England', Picador, 1990. Samuel Johnson: James Boswell: 'Life of Johnson', OUP, 1998.James Joyce: 'Dubliners', Penguin, 1992. 'Ulysses', Penguin, 1971. 'A Shorter Finnegan's Wake', ed. Anthony Burgess, 1985. Laurie Lee: 'Cider with Rosie', Hogarth Press, 1959. 'As I Walked Out One Midsummer Morning', Andre Deutsch, 1969. Jack London: 'John Barleycorn' Oxford, 1998. 'Martin Eden', Penguin, 1984. Alex Kershaw: 'Jack London. A Life', Flamingo, Harper Collins, 1998. Malcolm Lowry: 'Under the Volcano', Jonathan Cape, 1967. 'Ultramarine', Penguin, 1980. Gordon Bowker: 'Pursued by Furies. A Life of Malcolm Lowry', Harper Collins, 1993. Flann O'Brien: 'At Swim-Two-Birds', Penguin, 1990. 'The Best of Miles', Hart Davis MacGibbon, 1975. George Orwell: 'Collected Essays, Journalism and Letters of George Orwell', Secker & Warburg, 1949. '1984', Secker & Warburg, 1968.'Animal Farm', Secker & Warburg, 1945. 'A Clergyman's Daughter', Penguin, 1990. 'Keep the Aspidistra Flying', Penguin, 1963. William Shakespeare: 'The Complete Works of Shakespeare', Alexander Text, Collins, 1973.R L Stevenson: 'The Strange case of Dr Jekyll and Mr Hyde' Penguin, 2003. ' Everyman's Poetry. Robert Louis Stevenson', 1997. Jenni Calder: 'RLS. A Life Study', Hamish Hamilton, 1980. Dylan Thomas: 'Under Milk Wood', JM Dent, 1967. Paul Ferris: 'Dylan Thomas', Hodder & Stoughton, 1977. P G Wodehouse: 'Pigs Have Wings', Herbert Jenkins, 1952. 'The World of Mr Mulliner',

The author apologises for any errors or omissions in the above list and would be grateful to be notified of any corrections or copyright issues that should be addressed before the next edition of this volume.

INDEX

Flann O'Brien 2
Dylan Thomas 3
George Orwell 4
Robbie Burns 6
Chaucer 7
Shakespeare 8
Brendan Behan 10
Laurie Lee 11
Charles Dickens 12
Kingsley Amis 14
Jeffrey Bernard 15
Patrick Hamilton 17
Chesterton and Belloc 18
James Joyce 20
Ballads 21
More Ballads 22
Malcolm Lowry 24
Samuel Beckett 25
Dr. Johnson 27
Robert Louis Stevenson 28
Kenneth Grahame 30
P G Wodehouse 31
John Clare 33
Charles Bukowski 34
Pivo 35
Jack London 37
Thomas Hardy 38

FLANN O BRIEN

The Muses, said the Roman poet Horace, have usually smelt of drink first thing in the morning. And with that inspiring thought in mind let us go in search of the literary drinkers.

Drinking writers can be found lurking in cafes, restaurants or elegant society parties and very good places these are, but we shall confine ourselves to a more homely, but equally stimulating environment, the public house.

Writers are drawn to public houses, it seems, either for relief from the stresses of creation , or in search of material on which to work, or simply to find somebody tolerant or drunk enough to listen to their bursts of prejudice or egomania. Most writers are, it goes without saying, egomaniacs.

Let us start in Dublin, a city rightly famed for both its pubs and its writers. And having chosen Dublin, let us choose the author of At Swim-Two-Birds: Flann O Brien, or Myles na Gopaleen, or Brian O Nolan. Now there's a fine example of a drinking writer, a man who would take the elementary precaution of having three names, very useful for when some intrusive lover or creditor rings the pub and asks if you're in the bar. Whichever name they choose, you're the other one.

O Nolan (let's call him) was a central figure in the Bohemian Dublin of the 1950's, a friend of such writers (and drinking men) as Patrick Kavanagh and Brendan Behan. He was not, however, one of the wild men of Irish drinking legend. He was of a retiring disposition and there are surviving photographs of him immersed in a book while all around him fellow literary drinkers are waving their hats and arms in angry disputation. (CAMRA members, being instinctively cultured, may have experienced this phenomenon in this country, where to be found reading a book in some peaceful corner of a public house seems guaranteed to arouse frenzied hostility amongst the more unwashed locals.) There are also, I should concede, surviving pictures of O Nolan bawling and waving with the best of them.

He earned a fairly respectable living as a civil servant for many years, an unlikely profession on the face of it, a thought which after a while also occurred to his employers, who, baffled and occasionally outraged by his regular and satirical column in the Irish Times and his equally regular bouts of heavy drinking, did the honourable thing and fired him.

His fame rests in part on the above mentioned column called the Cruiskeen Lawn in which the immortal creation The Brother first drew breath (or porter). His forays into the theatre were less successful, but mention might here be made of a play interestingly entitled 'Thirst' of which an American critic remarked that it made drink more attractive than Oscar Wilde ever made lust.

But his enduring reputation is likely to derive from his novels, dripping with the absurdly comic and surreal language that he may have imbibed with the drink on his daily pub crawls along the Dublin quayside, in such bars as Mulligan's and the Scotch House, where he was known as the fuddled philosopher with a glass. Try 'The Third Policeman', an everyday village tale where a man turns into a bicycle, or what may be his masterpiece, 'At Swim-Two- Birds', in which a character declaims a rhyme that should hold an eternal truth for all of us:

> When things go wrong
> and will not come right
> Though you do the best you can
> When life looks black as the hour of night-
> A PINT OF PLAIN IS YOUR ONLY MAN

When money's tight and is hard to get
And your horse has also ran
When all you have is a heap of debt-
A PINT OF PLAIN IS YOUR ONLY MAN

As the speaker says, 'There are things in that pome that make for what you call permanence'.

DYLAN THOMAS

The Irish and the Scots are quite rightly famed for their drinking prowess, but the Welsh, the other Celtic race of the British Isles, are no strangers to the gargle themselves, as anyone who has hung around in Cardiff streets at closing time will testify. Therefore, remorselessly pushing back the boundaries of petty nationalism, the literary drinkers of 'Inspire' now move to deepest Wales, or more precisely Swansea and Laugharne, hosts to such Camraic delights as Buckleys and Brains. And there we find another writer much celebrated by literary drinkers, Dylan Thomas.

It is not merely his initials which commend him to our pages.

'Hush' says the first voice in his most famous work, 'Under Milk Wood', 'the babies are sleeping, the farmers, the fishers .... postman and publican, the undertaker and the fancy woman, drunkard, dressmaker, preacher, policeman, the webfoot cocklewomen and the tidy wives.'

And later in the play we make closer acquaintance with a couple of those figures from the beer drinking world. There is Mister Waldo, rabbitcatcher, whom the local gossips see 'falling in the gutter' and 'talking to the lamppost' and even 'using language'. A few vague memories stirred there, perhaps. More spectacularly follows Mr Cherry Owen who is described by his wife on the morning after the night before 'In you reeled, my boy, as drunk as a deacon with a big wet bucket and a fish frail full of stout and you looked at me and you said,' God has come home!' .... and then you took off your trousers and you said, 'Does anyone want a fight!' Perhaps not wholly surprising when we later learn that Cherry Owen's normal quota in The Sailor's Arms is 'seventeen pints of flat, warm, thin, Welsh, bitter beer'.

To be fair to Dylan Thomas, he seems to have been a man who lived from the inside the drinking world he portrays in his fiction. He was introduced to his interesting and energetic future wife, Caitlin Macnamara, in a London pub, The Wheatsheaf . It is to her memoirs that we owe much of our knowledge about Dylan Thomas's drinking habits.

We are told of his habit of lining up a string of light ales on the counter and downing them as a hangover cure, and of his fondness for pub games such as 'cats and dogs' in which he would go around on all fours barking and biting people's ankles. Try introducing that one to your local. It sounds a hoot.

He found in the seaside town of Laugharne, on which 'Under Milk Wood" was based, a beer drinker's idyll. His wife claimed it was a decadent place that never stopped drinking and that 'Under Milk Wood' was created from Brown's Hotel and what she sneeringly referred to as 'that flat Buckley's beer'. Since, however, her preferred tipple at the time was milk mixed with double whisky after which she used to throw herself off the harbour wall, we may perhaps doubt the validity of her judgements.

His American lecture tours did for Dylan Thomas in the end. He coped heroically with the attentions of American matrons whose lust for little fat Welshmen who smell of smoke apparently knew no bounds, but drew the line at American tastes in drink and would slip out of his hotel in New York to the White Horse Tavern, the nearest thing he could find to an English pub.

After his death in America, probably caused in part by his forced separation from the life-enhancing qualities of British beer, the legend continued. Even his coffin played its part, tracing an eccentric and circuitous route back from Southampton to Laugharne with a few pub stops on the way in Devon and Cornwall. It seems that his wake was a tribute to Welsh restraint in these matters. People fought and got senseless drunk all over town and some enterprising mourner had the initiative to sneak into his study and pinch a few of his manuscripts.

But we have enough of the man left in his fiction and in his letters to justify his inclusion in our hall of drinking fame. Let two of his remarks suffice. 'If I touched anything else but beer I just couldn't manage to get along' he said in a letter to his wife. And in a magnificent justification of his reputation as a great writer of love letters here is an irresistible invitation to a Welsh actress of his acquaintance: 'Perhaps you would come out with me, watch me drink a pint, and talk and talk and talk. Would you like that?' What decent woman could resist.

GEORGE ORWELL

An Irishman, a Welshman - about time for an Englishman in our literary drinking hall of fame . And our latest recruit, George Orwell, is quintessentially English. His real name was Eric Blair. He seems to have adopted his pen name out of some undefined need to separate himself from his past and to ally himself with a concept of Englishness. This was symbolised in his choice of Christian name and a surname taken from the Suffolk river flowing close to Adnams Brewery in Southwold where he lived for many years.

Orwell was not, like the previous subjects of this column, a destructive drinker, but a thoughtful , reflective observer of beers and places that sell beer, all in the service of his rather conservative nostalgia for the traditions of his native land. Rather like John Major, perhaps, but with intelligence.

In an essay for The Evening Standard he created a famous and enduring image of the ideal English pub which he called 'The Moon Under Water'. Most of its features seem to me unarguably admirable:

'Its clientele, though fairly large, consists mostly of regulars who occupy the same chair every evening and go there for conversation as much as for the beer. . . . . the barmaids know most of their customers by name, and take a personal interest in everyone. .. it is always quiet enough to talk. . ."

Orwell does make some rather unsettling remarks about the delights of hearing children's squeals as a background to steady supping, but I suppose we are all allowed our idiosyncrasies. In another less well-known essay he bemoans the fact that ' the pub as a cultural institution is at present declining' and cheers himself up by considering ' the complex social code that differentiates the saloon bar from the public bar, or . . . the delicate ritual that centres around treating, or the cultural implications of the trend towards bottled beer.'

In his book 'The English People', published in 1947, he inveighs against the imbecility of the licensing laws (plus ca change . .) and gains some grim satisfaction from the thought that ' the fanatics have been able to see to it that the Englishman drinks his glass of beer under difficulties and with a faint feeling of wrong-doing, but have not actually been able to prevent him from drinking it.'

Orwell's reputation probably (just) rests on his fiction. In this also an appreciation of the worth and significance of beer drinking comes through. In his political fable 'Animal Farm' the pigs celebrate their total assumption of power with beer and earlier sow the animals' retirement paddock with barley and change one of the farm commandments to ' No animal shall drink alcohol - to excess.'

In '1984', the doomed hero, Winston Smith, goes in search of evidence of the past. All he can find is an old working man who bewails the loss of imperial measures and its effect on his drinking habits:

'I likes a pint,' persisted the old man. 'You could 'a drawed me off a pint easy enough. We didn't 'ave these bleeding litres when I was a young man.'

In this vision of a future totalitarian state, Orwell had the good sense to portray interference in drinking habits as symptomatic of a desire to curtail all human freedoms.

"Keep the Aspidistra Flying' presents the sordid money-grabbing world of thirties England. Poverty's sharp bite is exemplified in the hero's inability to buy himself a beer: 'Oh, for a pint of beer! He seemed almost to feel it going down his throat. If only he had had any money! Even sevenpence for a pint.'

Later, nearly penniless and alone on the London streets , he finds himself shut outside that symbol of human warmth and companionship, the public house:

'The saloon bar was crowded. Like all rooms seen from the outside, it looked ineffably cosy. The fire that blazed in the grate danced, mirrored, in the brass spittoons. Gordon thought he could almost smell the beer through the glass.' The pity of it wrings the heart-strings.

Orwell, a true student of the art of brewing, was not merely a consumer; he was interested in the process itself. In 'A Clergyman's Daughter', Dorothy's wanderings lead her to the hop-picking fields of Kent: 'a scene somehow peaceful and alluring. The hop bines, tall climbing plants like runner beans enormously magnified, grew in green leafy lanes with the hops dangling from them in pale green bunches like gigantic grapes.'

From the beginning to the end of the brewing process, Orwell did for beer what French writers did for wine, established it as the national drink of England.

ROBERT BURNS

Of all the saccharine exercises in emasculated folksy self-indulgence that threaten to reduce The British Isles to the status of a theme park, Burns' Night must be up there with the worst.

Perhaps that's a bit harsh.

On the other hand the spectacle of ranks of White Heather Show extras patting their tartan trews in an orgy of middle class and middle brow self congratulation, all the while concentrating with whisky-induced difficulty on a gobful of theatrically declaimed verses is enough to turn any reasonable literary drinker to – well – drink.

This is rough justice on Robbie Burns, the unwitting source of all this sentimental gush. Not only was he a poet of far greater complexity than the kilt and haggis industry will allow, but he was as appreciative of the virtues of social drinking as he was of that other great human passion with which he and his poems are more usually associated. Thus, since Burns' Night has safely passed, let's make an overdue visit to Scotland, land of 'Trainspotting' and tartan, Belhaven and Broughton's, to encounter the latest of our literary drinkers.

It has been said that Scottishness is largely a state of mind. If so, it's a fairly bibulous one, at least in literary circles. Even a relatively minor Scots poet, Sidney Smith, took pride in adopting the title 'the boozy bard of Auld Reekie'. His celebration of beer extended to querying the drinking preferences of English Romantic poets

'Did Johnnie Keats when he was drouth,
Ask 'A beaker full o the warm South'?
Fegs no, he leaned across the bar,
An called for "A pint o bitter, Ma!"

Hugh MacDiarmud's most famous poem is 'A Drunk Man Looks at the Thistle'. In it he imagines himself drinking with Burns, who has left Edinburgh in disgust, 'To booze wi' thieveless cronies sic as me.'

Further back in drinking time William Dunbar wrote memorably of a pair of 15th century harpies fuelling their scorn of their menfolk with heavy drinking.

'Drynkand the wyne satt cumeris (gossips) tway'.

But I digress. Back to Burns. 'Gude ale keeps my heart aboon (high)' he wrote, but he knew the down side too. In a letter to a friend he spoke of the hangover-induced 'hounds of hell that beset a poor wretch who has been guilty of the sin of drunkenness.' His biographers tell us that the poor boy had a bad head for drink, but at least he seems to have had the decency to give it his best shot. Burns talks of a drinking contest amongst his friends where the victor apparently put away eight bottles of claret. While working in Dumfries he called on a friend who complained that 'he was half drunk when he came and completely drunk before he went away in the morning'.

Another friend took him out for a bracing horse ride during which they were caught in a downpour, after which according to the friend ' to revenge ourselves Burns insisted on our getting utterly drunk'. Later, in a letter, Burns admitted to a suspicion that 'some of our folks have conceived a prejudice against me as being a drunken dissipated character'. Beasts.

'Occasional hard drinking is the devil to me ... taverns I have totally abandoned,' he claimed, but that didn't last. Indeed we find him celebrating the virtues of the innkeeper Johnnie Pigeon, to whom

'Strong ale was ablution
Small beer persecution'

Burns' death, in fact, is popularly supposed to have occurred after a heavy drinking bout in a tavern.

If Burns understood anything, it was the concept of social drinking. He poured out

many drinking songs such as 'Willie Brew'd a Peck o' Maut' in which his characters cry out
> 'We are na fou (drunk), we're nae that fou, But just a drappie in our e'e . . .'

The usual disclaimer, in fact.

'Tam O' Shanter is a magnificent poem and it has a magnificent opening. In a bar, as the day comes to a long-awaited end,
> 'We sit bousing at the nappy (ale)
> And getting fou and unco happy'

Tam is nagged by his aleophobe wife who 'nurses her wrath to keep it warm', but he finds welcome solace in the company of his boozing chums. Later in the tale after he leaves the ale-house he defies and defeats through drunken bravado an even more malevolent series of hags in the shape of a shower of witches, apparently fresh from a production of 'Macbeth'. Thus, as often in Burns' poetry, liberty, good fellowship and drinking go hand in hand. As he said 'Freedom and whisky gang together'. Freedom, perhaps, even from such things as Burns' Nights.

GEOFFREY CHAUCER

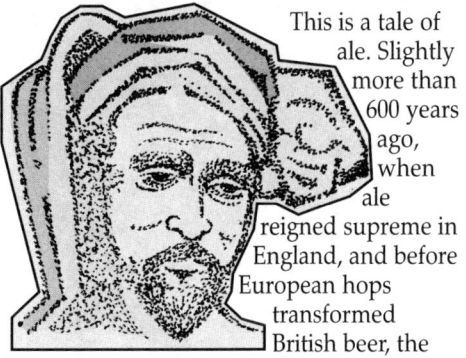

This is a tale of ale. Slightly more than 600 years ago, when ale reigned supreme in England, and before European hops transformed British beer, the first great classical work of English literature was being written. Geoffrey Chaucer's 'Canterbury Tales' begins in an inn, where a group of pilgrims meet up to travel to Canterbury:
> Bifil that in that seson on a day
> In Southwerk at the Tabard as I lay . .
> At night was come into that hostelrie
> Wel nine and twenty in a compaignie

After they set off on their travels, they take the world of the inn with them, both in the company of the landlord (The Host) who accompanies them, and in the tales they tell. This is not surprising. In the Middle Ages drinking water was often an interesting form of suicide. Ale, malt and water mixed, was a staple liquid diet. Festivals throughout the year were celebrated with special brews: help ales, christening ales and bride ales amongst others. In fact, ale became a standard around which the Eurosceptics of the day rallied. Henry VI issued an edict prohibiting brewers from using hops. Much ale was brewed at home and commercial brewing, largely an urban practice, was infested with crooks and shysters. Plus ca change . .

In 'The Harrowing of Hell', a medieval mystery play, a special place is kept in hell for brewers:
> 'taverners that are cunning
> Misspending much malt, brewing so thin,
> Selling small cups, money to win
> Against all truth to deal.'

Monasteries, of course, also cultivated brewing. It was their practice which introduced the custom of marking beer barrels with X, XX or XXX according to strength. In the Middle Ages the church was not the virulent opponent of social drinking that it became in later times. Many of Chaucer's most enthusiastic drinkers are to be found amongst his clerical pilgrims. The Friar ' knew the tavernes wel in every toune / And everich hostiler and tappestere'. A tappestere, by the way, as the suffix suggests was a female tapster, whose duties often stretched to more interesting and energetic pastimes than ale--pouring. The Summoner, a repellent and disfigured officer of the ecclesiastic courts, is permanently drunk and dressed appropriately:
> A gerland hadde he set upon his heed
> As greet as it were for an ale-stake.

(An ale-stake, for those imbued with a passionate thirst for knowledge, was a long pole with a bundle of branches bound on the end, stuck up outside an ale-house.)

The Pardoner, another cleric and an interestingly close friend of the Summoner, tells a tale set in an ale-house, and insists that ' heere at this alestake / I wol both drinke, and eten of a cake,' before he agrees to begin his story. Ironically he opens his tale with a diatribe against drunkenness:

dronkenesse
Is full of striving and of wrecchednesse.
O dronke man, disfigured is thy face
Sour is thy breeth, foul artow to embrace. . .

Hands up all those who have been welcomed home with similar endearments.

The clerics don't have it all their own way on the road to Canterbury, however. The Miller gets 'dronke of ale' and pushes his way in front of his social betters to tell his tale. His enemy and rival, the Reeve tells a tale about a miller who makes the big mistake of letting a couple of students lodge for the night in his house.

The students and their host 'drinken ever strong ale atte best, Aboute midnight wente they to reste'. The miller, by now 'pale he was for-dronken' sleeps heavily throughout the night while the students get their scholastic legs over his wife and daughter.

Another pilgrim, the Cooke, seems to have a thirst characteristic of those who work in hot surroundings 'Wel coude he knowe a draught of London ale', and one way and another it is surprising that Chaucer's set of drinking pilgrims ever actually made it to Canterbury.

That they did is probably a tribute to the Host, the landlord of the inn from which they set out and their self-appointed guide and leader. He is almost certainly based on a real life innkeeper called Harry Bailey who would have been a London neighbour of the poet. In what passes for real life, landlords are seldom the stuff that dreams are made of, but Chaucer's Host comes close. Pubs today still have something in common with Chaucer's Tabard Inn, places where weary pilgrims of many social and moral shapes and sizes can rest for a while and drink their ale before being kicked out onto an unpredictable and hostile world.

WILLIAM SHAKESPEARE

"Dost thou think, because thou art virtuous, there shall be no more cakes and ale?"

Students of beer will know that Renaissance England witnessed some seminal events in the history of English brewing. In particular, the battle to preserve native ale at the expense of hopped beer seems finally to have been lost. In such vibrant and contentious times, it is not surprising that the great English writers of the time turned their attentions to beer and beerhouses.

It was an an inebriated age: it seems likely that much of the adult male population of sixteenth century London was permanently under the influence. The Thames was considered sweet enough to drink, but the practice was to sup small beer at breakfast. Philip Stubbes, a notoriously miserable sod, ranted against the prevalence of heavy drinking: ' a man once drunk rather resembleth a brute than a Christian man. For do not his eyes begin to stare and be red, fiery and bleared, blubbering forth seas of tears? Doth he not froth and foam at the mouth like a boar?' Well, I suppose, now you mention it . . .

As in most matters, however, Shakespeare found much to celebrate in this quintessentially human activity. Iago, a serpentine Venetian in the tragedy of 'Othello' finds time in his plotting to make awed reference to English drinking habits: 'I learned it [a drinking song] in England, where indeed they are most potent in potting. Your Dane, your German, and your swag-bellied Hollander - are nothing to your English.'

Falstaff, fat and flamboyant, emerged from that fictional Eden of taverns, the Boar's Head, to dominate the plays in which he appeared. He represented for the theatre-going Elizabethans the triumph of natural man against the forces of narrow respectability [no straitlaced middle-class audiences in Shakespeare's theatre].

'Shall I,' he thundered, speaking for all of us, badgered by officialdom and oafish vulgarity, ' not take mine ease in mine inn?'

Shakespeare's interest in taverns and what goes on inside them is not surprising, bearing in mind that the shape of the English Theatre clearly derives out of the shape of the Elizabethan inn: a square yard enclosed by an upper gallery. Beer would be sold in the theatres in plenty; the story goes that when Shakespeare's Globe burned down in 1613, one of the audience had his burning breeches doused with ' pottled ale'.

The relative prices of these pleasures make interesting reading: it has been calculated that a quart of ale was more expensive than a high priced ticket at the public theatres.

Certainly the monarch appreciated her beer. The Earl of Leicester had no ale strong enough for her at Hatfield: 'we were fain to send to London . . her own bere was so strong as there was no man able to drink it.' Shakespeare himself knew enough about the priorities of the times to have stored malt in his house in Stratford in 1598 after the dearth of previous years.

Another, more satirical, Elizabethan dramatist, Ben Jonson, explored the vices of the time through attention to the habits of those who drank and sold beer. In his play 'Bartholemew Fair' the unscrupulous landlady, Ursula, gives some revealing advice to her tapster (barman): 'Froth your cans well in the filling, rogue and jog your bottles o' the buttock . . but your true trick, rascal, must be ever busy and mis-take away the bottles and cans in haste before they be half drunk off, and never hear anybody call till you ha' brought fresh and be able to foreswear 'em.' Hands up those who recognise the great-great grandmother of their local barstaff.

But the Elizabethans were a positive people. Let's finish with John Earle's famous praise of the English tavern , from his encyclopaedic work 'Microcosmographie':

''the busy man's recreation, the idle man's business, the melancholy man's sanctuary, the stranger's welcome, the scholar's kindness and the citizen's courtesy. It is the study of sparkling wits.' Amen.

BRENDAN BEHAN

Farewell to the foothills of literary drinking. It is time to keep company with one of the immortals, a truly heroic drinker, a man who once described himself as 'a drinker with a writing problem'.

Brendan Behan was not a man to take himself or his drinking lightly. He became a walking art form of his own creation and, in true Celtic fashion, his creation rose up and slew him. He was born in Dublin in 1923.When aged 16 he was arrested in connection with his involvement with the IRA; three years later he was sentenced to 14 years for shooting at a policeman, and less than a year after being released he got a month with hard labour for assaulting another officer of the law.

In his later life, however, he concentrated his attention on activities, which if not a great deal more peaceful, were at least legal: drinking and writing. It would be stretching matters to describe Behan as one of life's discriminating drinkers, but he had a well attested fondness for the black stuff. He was once described as being ' like a barrel of porter : full of goodness, heady, not to be taken in excess and with sediment that should not be stirred up'. In 'Brendan Behan's Island' he bewailed the recent decline in porter drinking, recalling a time when the drink 'was so good that the glass it was in used to stick to the counter'. It is doubtful whether he would have had much sympathy for recent drinking fashions such as the plague of Irish theme bars or the obsession with serving Guinness at temperatures low enough to appeal to lager drinkers.

Irish pubs have traditionally answered a range of complex social needs, perhaps even more so than in Great Britain. Behan was their chronicler and historian. In 'Hold Your Hour and Have Another' he parades before us a glittering succession of pub characters : Red Jam Roll, Whacker Kinsella, Duck the Bullet and mad Mrs Mountpenny who thought she was a lobster. In what is generally thought of as his best play, 'The Quare Fellow', two of the characters define misery and salvation in terms of opening hours:

'Neighbour: Only then to wake up on some lobby and the hard floorboards under you, and a lump of hard filth for your pillow, and the cold and the drink shaking you, wishing it was morning for the market pubs to open, where if you had the price of a drink you could sit in the warm anyway. Except, God look down on you, if it was Sunday.

Dunlavin: Ah, there's the agony. No pub open, but the bells battering your bared nerves and all you could do with the cold and the sickness was to lean over on your side and wish that God would call you.'

Behan was equally knowing and informative about American bars. In 'Brendan Behan's New York' he rambles through Costello's where Hemingway had left a shillelagh snapped in two in a test of strength and McSorley's, where if a woman happened to gain entrance a ship's bell was rung and she was instantly ejected.

Readers of Brendan Behan's books have turned - reasonably - to drinking metaphors to do them justice. A review of 'Richard's Cork Leg' - the source of this rather eccentric title is worth finding out, by the way - claimed that the play had ' all the theatrical significance of a pint of ale - sometimes full of yeasty ferment, sometimes merely full of boozy conviviality.' Louis MacNeice (another good drinking Irish writer) applauded 'Brendan Behan's Island' as 'a book which he who drinks may read.'

Bacchus is a remorselessly even-handed deity, however. He tends to weigh out pain and pleasure in scrupulously balanced doses. Hence the hangover, I suppose. Behan's final years were flamboyantly celebratory, but the celebrations were of the 'last orders' variety.

During the first West End production of 'The Hostage', Behan occupied himself by snatching the hat from a busker performing outside Wyndham's Theatre, putting on his own performance and returning a well-filled hat to the busker. He was present during the opening of 'The Hostage' in San Francisco. In the course of the play he poured a bottle of stout over actors and audience, sang 'I was Lady Chatterley's Lover' and dragged one of the actors offstage and took him to the bar.

His last attempts to dry out were strikingly unsuccessful. Dublin pubs are notorious graveyards for real or aspiring geniuses. Patrick Kavanagh, a poet and contemporary of Behan's, was to die of drink-related illness, as was an earlier subject of this column, Flann O'Brien. We shall let the latter have the last words, taken from the obituary he wrote for the Sunday Telegraph:

'a reckless drinker, a fearless denouncer of humbug and pretence . . . there are streets in Dublin which seem strangely silent tonight.'

LAURIE LEE

One of the most heart-rending sounds of recent years has been the bewildered wail of innocence put up by the drinks industry when accused of promoting under-age drinking. Perhaps their bottles *are* garishly decorated in juvenile colours. Maybe the alcohol content *is* disguised by fizzy sweetness. Possibly the advertising campaigns *do* tend to offer up images of spurious sophistication to the gauche and adolescent. But that brewers would deliberately . . . . ? Hard to believe.

Earlier periods in English history provided drinking initiation ceremonies that did not require the participants to resort to such squalid effluent as alcopop. And there were side benefits. Laurie Lee's famous autobiography, 'Cider With Rosie', gives due prominence to his discovery of two of the more obvious compensations for our being saddled with humanity.

"It's cider," she said. "You ain't to drink it though. Not much of it, any rate."
'Huge and squat, the jar lay on the grass like an unexploded bomb. We lifted it up, unscrewed the stopper and smelt the whiff of fermented apples . . .
"Go on," said Rosie . . . . Never to beforgotten that first long secret drink of golden fire, juice of those valleys and of that time, wine of wild orchards, of Rosie's burning cheeks . . . her husky, perilous whisper drugged me, and the cider beat gongs in my head.'

Laurie Lee is perhaps the most famous celebrant of the delights of 'real' cider, a drink which the Tudor writer Thomas Elyot claimed was the cause of those who drank it having 'the skin of their visage rivelled although that they be young.' In more recent times cider has tended to be linked in popular mythology with waste ground and challenging mixers such as meths.

Laurie Lee's drinking credentials, however, extend to more than redeeming the reputation of cider.

Some sixty years after the events chronicled above he had become something of a fixture in The Woolpack, a 16th century pub in the Slad Valley in Gloucestershire where 'Cider With Rosie' is set. Showing due

Illustration by Mike Cornford

deference to its famous resident, The Woolpack, in addition to such delights as Uley Old Spot, offered its customers Weston Old Rosie Cider. History does not record whether Old Rosie was still on hand to offer reminders of her earlier favours.

Laurie Lee came from a family well practised in drinking matters. His grandfather ran The Plough, a small local inn, and his mother was soon summoned to join him. The young Lee drank in ' days of rough brews, penny ales, tuppenny rums, home-made cider, the staggers and violence'. His grandfather's definition of running a pub, it seems, was to leave it to his daughter while he 'spent his time in the cellar playing the fiddle'. Makes a change from incessant holidays in Minorca.

Spain, in fact, was where Laurie Lee memorably ended up, having left home at the age of nineteen to tramp the world. While there, as his book 'As I Walked Out On A Midsummer Morning' recounts, he fell in with a pot-pourri of drinkers, from German students 'noisily drinking the warm local beer' to an unending string of Spaniards in small local bars 'designed for quieter, more twilit drinking'.

Outside one such bar he met another writer and another epic drinker, the South African poet Roy Campbell. Campbell temporarily adopted the young man, which may not have done much for his chances of following the path of abstinence.

Campbell was the man who established a fearsome drinking reputation in post-war London, often in the company of Dylan Thomas. (q.v). They used to meet in The Catherine Wheel in Camden Road where to while away a session on one St. David's Day the poetical pair consumed for a bet a bunch of daffodils, stalks and all..

Anyway, back to Laurie Lee. After his European wanderings he also ended up in the Bohemian world of 50's London. There he mixed with some fairly exalted drinking company and apparently made quite an impact. Jeffrey Bernard (q.v) used to date events in the 50's by calculating how long a certain event was from 'the last time Laurie Lee bought a drink.'

He became a famous, and it seems not altogether reluctant, celebrity in the bars of both London and - after returning home - Slad. As his account of the Gloucestershire countryside brought him fame, so his celebration of the potency of a too often undervalued drink has enshrined him forever in drinking lore.

CHARLES DICKENS

'There was plenty going on at the brewery, and the reek and the smell of grains, and the rattling of the plump dray horses at their mangers were capital company. Quite refreshed by having mingled with this good society, I made a new start with a new heart.'

Charles Dickens wrote this tribute to the sensuous delights of the brewing industry in 1860. It is an extract from a piece of journalism called 'Night Walks', in which Dickens records his wanderings at night through the streets of London. He observes people as well as places, especially drinking people, at the time 'when the late public houses turned their lamps out, and when the potmen thrust the last brawling drunkards into the street'. He notes how 'if we were lucky, a policeman's rattle sprang and a fray turned up', but bewails the fact that 'in general, surprisingly little of this diversion was provided'. A judicious sampling of certain South Derbyshire villages of today might have cured his disappointment.

Nevertheless, after some caustic remarks about 'a regular species of drunkard, the thin-armed, puff-faced, leaden-lipped gin drinker', he finds satisfaction in more beery behaviour, in particular the way in which 'intoxicated people appeared to be magnetically attracted towards each other:

so that we knew when we saw one drunken object stagggering against the shutters of a shop, that another drunken object would stagger up before five minutes were out, to fraternise or fight with it.'

The world of journalism is not normally associated with total abstinence, and so it is not surprising that Dickens shows a keen interest in drinking matters, but as it is his novels which brought him his most lasting fame, so it is his celebrated fictional drinkers that best show his worthiness to be included in any list of literary drinkers.

In 'A Tale of Two Cities', that queen of harridans, Madame Defarge, is the wife of a wine-shop keeper, which may have given her the taste for another red liquid. An even more famous character from the novel is Sydney Carton. In addition to embracing his own death as a good thing, Carton has gone down in literary history as one of the great heroic drinkers, a man who when he met the aristocrat for whom he was later to sacrifice himself (a sad waste, I should have said) 'smelt of port wine, and did not appear to be quite sober'. We are later told, to increase our admiration, that what carton and his legal partner 'drank together, between Hilary Term and Michaelmas, might have floated a king's ship'. But as Dickens points out earlier in the novel, 'Those were drinking days, and most men drank hard.'

They appear to have drunk hard in most of Dickens's other novels too. In 'Barnaby Rudge' much of the action centres around an inn called The Maypole, and Dickens reasonably observes 'how unnatural it seemed for a sober man to be plodding wearily along through miry roads' when close at hand were ' a well-swept hearth, a blazing fire, bright pewter flagons' and all the other accoutrements of a well-kept tavern. Later in the novel, however, hordes of drunken rioters invade the inn, and their leader, Hugh, subjects John the Landlord to any publican's worst nightmare:
"These lads are thirsty and must drink! " cried Hugh . .

John faintly articulated the words, 'Who's to pay?'
"He says, 'Who's to pay?'" cried Hugh, with a roar of laughter which was loudly echoed by the crowd. Then turning to John, he added, "Pay? Why, nobody."

Shocking.

'The Old Curiosity Shop' is in many ways typical Dickens. It contains a ludicrous child-heroine in Little Nell, one of the crew that John Carey called Dickens's 'antiseptic, expurgated dwarfs'. Luckily, it also has Quilp, who as usual with Dickens's villains is a far more credible (even admirable) creature. The novel also presents to us one of Dickens's many roguish and eccentric young men, Dick Swiveller. It is he who meets an even more subordinate servant, a female whom for some obscure reason he christens the Marchioness. Having met her, he quite reasonably proceeds to interrogate her about her drinking habits.
"Did you ever taste beer?"
" I had a sip of it once," said the small servant.
" Here's a state of things!" cried Mr Swiveller, raising his eyes to the ceiling. " She never tasted it – it can't be tasted in a sip!"

Quite right, of course.

The greatest of Dickens's servants, though, is Sam Weller of 'The Pickwick Papers', that immortal celebration of drinking tours. In addition to guiding his master through the pleasures and perils of his drinking Odyssey, Sam Weller protects Pickwick against the multitude of villains, comic and otherwise, who cross their path. Amongst these is the peerless Mr Stiggins, a preacher whose fulminations against the demon drink are only matched by his capacity for it.

"Wot's your usual tap,sir?" replied Sam. "Oh, my dear young friend," replied Mr Stiggins, " all taps is vanities! . . I despise them all. If," said Mr Stiggins, "if there is any one of them less odious than another, it is the liquor called rum. Warm, my dear young friend, with three lumps of sugar to the tumbler."'

Later, after consuming most of a bottle of port wine, Mr Stiggins 'conjured him to avoid above all things, the vice of intoxication. At this point the reverent gentleman became singularly incoherent, and staggering to and fro in the excitement of his eloquence, was fain to catch at the back of a chair to preserve his perpendicular.'

At the conclusion of his novels, Dickens tended to reward his more virtuous characters with some form of rustic retirement. It seems hugely appropriate that the Wellers, perhaps the greatest of Dickens's comic families, ended their days ' in an excellent public house near Shooter's Hill.'

KINGSLEY AMIS

However knowledgeable, even passionate, about drink our previous subjects may have been, none has written a book specifically about drinking.

Kingsley Amis has. His collection of essays 'On Drink' is in its own way regarded as a little gem. At different times he was commissioned to write articles on drink and drinking for The Telegraph Magazine and The Daily Express. He has also worked in the trade. During his time in Cambridge, when his famously toothed son Martin studied with some illustrious contemporaries at The Cambridgeshire High School for Boys, Amis served as the wine steward for Peterhouse College. In his later years he became a habitue of The Flask in Hampstead where one of his favourite quenchers was reportedly Youngs bitter and Ramrod. A subtle concoction.

Here is Amis, a man of some experience in these matters, discoursing on the perils of drinking firewater: 'I once shared a half-litre bottle of Polish Plain Spirit (140 proof) with two chums. I only spoke twice, first to say, 'Cut out that laughing- it can't have got to you yet,' and not all that much later to say, 'I think I'll go to bed now.'

Drink and drinking predictably played a significant part in his novels. Amis is often considered a very English writer. His letters for instance are full of the gleefully acerbic comments on English social mores that characterise a certain type of right wing Englishman. His fictional personae also allowed Amis to expound on the virtues of British brews. Here a character from 'I Like it Here' ignores the charms of a woman sitting on his lap: 'He soon began thinking about beer . . Although Portuguese beer tasted much less of bone-handled knives than other continental beers, it still wasn't as nice as English beer. . .He thought to himself now that if ever he went into the brewing business his posters would have written . .across the bottom in bold lettering the words 'Makes You Drunk.'

In his famous 1950's novel 'Lucky Jim', a satire against social and cultural pretensions, we have one of the most famous descriptions of a hangover in 20th century literature: 'He lay sprawled . . a dusty thudding in his head made the scene before him beat like a pulse. His mouth had been used as a latrine by some small creature of the night, and then as its mausoleum. During the night, too, he'd somehow been on a cross-country run and then been expertly beaten up by secret police. He felt bad.'

Generously, Amis also wrote at length on how to deal with a hangover. His advice deserves to be read more fully in the original, but suffice it to say here that his recommendations include vigorous sexual activity (on the presumption that your wife or partner is in the bed with you). He very properly advises against this procedure if you find yourself in bed with a stranger, on the grounds that this will merely exacerbate the feelings of guilt normally associated with hangovers. 'For the same generic reason,' Amis continues, 'do not take matters into your own hands if you awake by yourself.'

Looking further for sources of low comedy, Amis understandably turned to Wales, a country on which he had already delivered himself of several considered reflections, preserved in his collected letters. In one of these he declaims his desire to do verbal and physical violence to Dylan Thomas, an earlier subject of this series, and in another he comments on the 'incredible profusion of sexagenarian alcoholics' to be found in Wales.

In 'The Old Devils' a group of disenchanted old men hurl themselves into an extended drinking session around South Wales, and in the process of their decidedly un-Quixotic tour give Amis plenty of opportunity to make some dry observations about British drinking habits.

Here he is on two particularly repellent elements of pub life: first, piped music: 'generic sleepy lagoon muck full of swirls and tinkles,' and second, the pub bore: 'an old man had settled himself on a padded stool facing her and was going on as if he was a friend of them both by all means short of speech.'

They find a sort of refuge in the Bible and Crown, where they are able to drink copious amounts of Troeth bitter in a dingy bar where 'in winter the genial host actually let them have the benefit of a small electric fire at no extra cost.' If that latter statement takes some believing, then credibility is restored when the said landlord later turns on them and cast them into the outer darkness beyond the pub walls, with the cry familiar to many literary drinkers: 'I've been dying to get rid of you buggers for years.'

JEFFERY BERNARD

Picture in your mind the classic English pub. Small, low-ceilinged, cosy, possibly thatched, stone-floored and with a large walled garden. A country pub set in a traditional English village.

Most pubs, of course, are nothing like that. Most pubs are found in cities and most literary drinkers drink in city pubs. And most of these are in London.

Dr. Johnson (q.v.) famously celebrated taverns as being places of much happiness. Another famous literary celebrant of London pubs was Jeffrey Bernard. Happiness, however, was not really his subject. His 'Low Life' column in 'The Spectator', once memorably described as a suicide note in weekly instalments, triumphantly asserted the joys of being miserable and bringing misery to others. In the process he created two contenders for the titles of great English pubs and publicans.

An early CAMRA guide to London described The Coach and Horses in Soho as 'small, busy and basic'. Basic or not, Bernard took up triumphant residence there.

In his case the traditional valediction of the landlord 'Have you no homes to go to?' could not have been less appropriate. In his column a Hogarthian procession of more or less dissolute characters paraded themselves along the bar against which he leant his

15

stool. And behind the bar he pictured Norman, a paradigm of the curmudgeonly English landlord.

In answer to a spoof health questionnaire query as to whether drinking interfered with his work, he answered, 'The situation is very much the reverse. Work frequently interferes with my drinking….and another thing. Drinking is my work.' Bernard managed to become a literary and drinking institution, rather ironic for a man who claimed his philosophy of life was to 'aim low and miss'. He also seemed to have the knack of attracting desirable women, not a talent normally associated with professional drinkers.

The height of his celebrity came as a result of the play 'Jeffrey Bernard is Unwell' by Keith Waterhouse, another literary man with sound drinking credentials. In the play, the character Jeffrey Bernard finds himself locked in the Coach and Horses for the night. While passing the time getting peacefully plastered, he is visited by the voices of a series of acquaintances, past and present, living and dead. During the course of the evening he recalls the various people he's stumbled into in various gutters, where – he asserts – you find the best company. He attempts a version of his own obituary, but finds recall of detail problematic, not surprising from a man who having been asked to write his autobiography, penned a letter to the Spectator in which he asked if anyone could tell him what he was doing between 1960 and 1974. He muses on the rituals associated with pub drinking and considers the virtues of instituting an 'Unhappy Hour'.

Peter O'Toole, who memorably played the part in the first production, used to say that it was the role he'd been waiting for all his life. Bernard used to turn up in the theatre bar when the play was running, but seldom went to watch it on the reasonable grounds that he'd lived the thing in the first place.

The Independent's obituary described him as 'his own Boswell' and Bernard's writing does fall into that very English category of inconsequential, chatty diaries which somehow manage to act as chronicles of their age. Boswell quoted Dr Johnson as claiming that drink 'makes a man more pleased with himself. I do not say that it makes him more pleasing to others.' Bernard would have appreciated that. He talked, in a spoof obituary, of his arrival in Soho, and of how 'from that point he was never to look upward.' In fact one of his collections of essays was defiantly titled 'Reach for the Ground.'

Drink killed him in the end, but with characteristic defiance he wrote before he died that 'In my past, at my lowest ebbs, I used to think that maybe drink had destroyed my life, but that was dramatic nonsense and temporary gloom. Without alcohol, I would have been a shop assistant, a business assistant or a lone bachelor bank clerk. But why pick on bank clerks?'

PATRICK HAMILTON

Like any good campaigning periodical, 'Inspire' is fearless in its pursuit of truth and honesty. Honesty, therefore, compels us to concede that drink can have its downside. It goes without saying that no blame can be attached to drink itself. Nevertheless, the careers of literary drinkers have occasionally come to rather grisly grief. One such case is that of Patrick Hamilton.

Hamilton was born in Sussex, not far from Brighton, which is more often associated in literary terms with Graham Greene, and is of course itself much celebrated as a drinking haunt of variety and depth. Hamilton set 'The West Pier' in Brighton, but this strange, obsessive tale is oddly unconcerned with drinking matters. More typical is his memorable trilogy 'Twenty Thousand Streets Under the Sky', built around a Soho pub of the thirties, The Midnight Bell. The central characters of the novels are Bob, a waiter, and Ella, a barmaid. The trilogy opens with Bob suffering the drinker's familiar and painful surfacing into consciousness:

'He remembered coming up here, a happy man, at half-past three . . .He turned over with a sigh and a fresh spasm of sickness swept over him. He waited motionlessly and submissively until it passed. Then he cursed himself softly and vindictively. He faced facts. He had got drunk at lunch again.'

No-one has ever described pub life more vividly and accurately than Patrick Hamilton, no doubt due to the selfless way in which he devoted most of his life to visiting these places in pursuit of his literary researches. J.B. Priestly was perhaps thinking of this when he remarked that Hamilton 'spent too many of his years in an alcoholic haze', but conceded his genius in rendering 'the sheer idiocy of pub talk'. Doris Lessing, more generously, claimed that 'He wrote more sense about England and what was going on in England in the 1930s than anybody else I can think of, and his novels are true now. You can go into any pub and see it going on.'

Whatever the faults of pub life which Hamilton unblinkingly chronicled, the dark and malevolent world he depicted lurking outside the brightly lit saloon bars of his novels is far worse. Here again he may have drawn from experience. At the height of his fame he was knocked down and maimed by a motor car: a manifestation of social evil the equal of anything attributable to drink. His sexual life also seems to have been somewhat unsatisfactory. An affair with a London prostitute called Lily apparently generated more than the usual mixture of sado-masochism, and his first marriage is reported to have been a triumph of physical incompatibility. All this may have hurried him back to the bar. As a wise man once said: 'Beer never turns you down. Beer doesn't mind when you turn up. Beer doesn't complain if you spend time with other beers. Beer has no interest in home improvements.'

Hamilton's fictional world of loneliness, betrayal and seedy criminality emerges most powerfully in 'Hangover Square'. In this, perhaps his most famous novel, set in pre-war London, a crowd of vindictive barflies drink themselves steadily into oblivion. Their remorseless decline at least gives Hamilton the opportunity to muse on the surreal nature of a drinking life.

'It became clear to Johnnie that they were all going to get drunk . . so he resigned himself to the joys of alcohol, wisely telling himself that if there was to be a hateful and repentant morning after the night before, he would at least see that the pleasure of the night was not marred by the hatefulness of repentance . . . Johnnie always thought that of you could only have your morning after first, and your night before after wards, the whole problem of drinking, and indeed of excess and sin in life generally, would be simplified or solved.' Wise words.

He spent his last years in Norfolk, having earlier discovered the delights of the pubs of Wells-next-the-Sea and the rightly celebrated Lord Nelson in Burnham. His brother was as brothers should be, a life-long admirer and friend, and the recipient of Hamilton's many letters concerning his attempts to control his drinking. Here is an excerpt from one written when he was theoretically on the wagon:

'My dearest Bruce –the time is eight o'clock
I'm sitting up in bed and drinking Bock.
At least, not Bock, but ordinary beer,
Which is the only stuff they give you here.
At least, not beer, but Hammerton's brown stout
Useful for milder kinds of drinking bout.'

In the end he managed to drink himself to death, but what killed him made him famous. Let us conclude with his description of the quintessential landlord and landlady, taken from 'The Midnight Bell':

'the Governor and his wife made no attempt at divergence from type. They were as benign as they were bloated. It was pretty obvious to everybody that they might both burst at any moment, but this fact seemed to contribute to rather than detract from their unvarying benevolence.'

G. K. CHESTERTON & HILAIRE BELLOC

It has been pointed out by many avid 'Innspire' readers (thank you, Sven and Olaf of Spitsbergen) that in recent months this column has tended to dwell on the darker side of drinking and failed to give due emphasis to the humble delights of bathing oneself in ale. We hear and are accordingly chastened. Step forward, therefore, Hilaire Belloc, and step forward with him, if 'step' does not suggest too sprightly a gait, his friend and drinking partner, G.K.Chesterton.

George Bernard Shaw depicted then as a single monstrous figure called 'Chesterbelloc', and photographs of Chesterton show him as a Matterhorn of a man, a physical tribute to years of determined beer drinking. Belloc may be most commonly associated with his 'Cautionary tales', satisfyingly gruesome poems in which poisonous and priggish middle-class brats for once (c.f. C.S. Lewis) get their rightful come-uppance. His association with Chesterton was based on a range of mutual interests, including what seemed to be a particularly virulent form of anti-semitism, but also, and more relevantly for our purposes, a devotion to drinking beer.

Belloc and Chesterton met in Soho, a very appropriate spot for an encounter between drinking men. From that time on heavy drinking became something of a point of honour in the literary set which grew up around them.

Sausages and beer were apparently the basis of all sessions conducted under Chesterton's hospitality. Both men wrote widely in a variety of forms; both men wrote a great deal about Southern England and its ale.

There is, for instance, Chesterton's 'The Rolling English Road' which famously opens with:

'Before the Romans came to Rye or out to Severn strode,
The rolling English drunkard made the rolling English road.'

The speaker claims he went to fight the French because they came:

'To straighten out the crooked road an English drunkard made
Where you and I went down the lane with ale-mug in our hands,
The night we went to Glastonbury by way of Goodwin Sands.'

And these lines are from Belloc's 'A Sussex Drinking Song':

When branch is bare in Burton Glen,
And Bury Hill is a whitening, then,
I drink strong ale with gentlemen ;

And in a regional self-definition, the poem's persona continues:

We are of the stout South Country stuff,
That never can have good ale enough,

Denial, or self-denial did not figure largely in either man's make-up. Unlike many writers, Chesterton claimed he wrote easily under the influence of drink. As mentioned above, he was an imposing physical specimen, largely due to the unfashionable combination of maximum beer intake and minimal exercise. Shaw asserted that he became bigger as you looked at him. One story describes him, short of funds and thirsty, working in the British Museum. Desperate for a drink, he drew a picture of a man suffering from the pangs of hunger, passed it round and then made off to the pub with the collection.

Marriage slowed him down for a while. His wife took him off to Beaconsfield in Buckinghamshire where he penned these words in a lament for his lost drinking companions:

'When I came back to Fleet Street,
Through a sunset nook at night,
And saw the old Green Dragon
With the windows all alight,
And hailed the old Green Dragon,
And the Cock I used to know,
Where all good fellows were my friends,
A little while ago . . .

Tear-jerking. And, of course, his exile didn't work; it simply turned him into a solitary drinker, so there's a cautionary tale for us all. He still found time to write 'The Flying Inn', in which England is governed by Moslem law and the central character circumvents the drinking laws by turning his pub into a mobile beer-serving station. He travelled widely, went to America and found the Americans 'delighted to discuss it (prohibition) over the nuts and the wine. They were even willing, if necessary, to dispense with the nuts.'

Chesterton died in 1936. In his compelling fantasy 'The Man Who Was Thursday' the central God-like character finally asks, 'Can ye drink of the cup that I drink of?' In his poem 'The English People' he drifts back to the 17th century where: 'a few men talked of freedom, while England talked of ale.'

In 'The Rolling English Road' Chesterton had envisioned 'the decent inn of death'. It sounds a suitable final resting place.

JAMES JOYCE

James Joyce once called Ireland:
'This lovely land that always sent
Her writers and artists to banishment
And in a spirit of Irish fun
Betrayed her own leaders, one by one'

Ireland took her revenge by delaying the publication of his works and - as Joyce saw it - driving him into exile. It is therefore wholly appropriate, in an Irish sort of way, that a statue of Joyce now adorns O'Connell Street and that Joycean literary tours play a central part in Ireland's tourist industry. Irish theme pubs, which seem to have spread like a stream of effluent across Europe, are no less eager to use Joyce's name. If you go into Hannigan's bar in Granada, in amongst the agricultural implements and adverts for Guinness, you will find a portrait of James Joyce looking down at you with rather a patrician air.

If Joyce's face has to be used to sell anything, it might as well be drink. He once described himself as ' a man of small virtue, inclined to extravagance and alcoholism.' These words might equally be applied to his father. John Joyce was a man of wide acquaintance and deep thirst. His sustained and flamboyant exercises in public and private drunkenness are well chronicled by various members of his family. When informed of the name of his son's bride, Nora Barnacle, he is said to have remarked that there was a girl who would stick to you. More to the point, she turned out to be a glittering example of why Irish women are rightly venerated: their appreciation that heavy drinking is a natural occupation for a man.

Joyce's own brother Stanislaus, not being a drinking man himself, was not unreservedly kind to drunks, and his biography 'My Brother's Keeper', describes how he spent his time hunting James down and dragging him out of bars in Dublin, Trieste and Rome. Joyce's behaviour on these occasions was often exotic. He was given to performing odd spiderish dances in the street, in which he flailed his long arms and legs about with some abandon. As his daughter-in-law put it, 'Liquor went to his feet, not head.'

Joyce apparently started off his drinking career with sack, in an attempt at aping the Elizabethans, but soon moved on to porter. He used to taunt his brother with Blake's line ' the road of excess leads to the palace of wisdom'. Stanislaus bitterly concluded that his revels might at least well qualify him to be an effective chronicler of Dublin, 'that sottish capital'.

And that is what Joyce became. As Anthony Burgess said, 'Joyce's purpose in life was to glorify the Dublin of pubs and poverty, not to further a shining national image.' To follow the development of his craft as a writer is to discover that consistency of vision. 'Counterparts', a marvellous short story from 'Dubliners', reeks of the warm sweaty air of the public bar. The central character is a hulking office clerk who spends his time resentfully chained to his desk yearning for ' a good night's drinking . . . amid the glare of gas and the clatter of glasses.' After a confrontation in the office he feels 'his great body again aching for the comfort of the public house' to which he goes, but not with happy results.

'Ulysses' is an elaborate interweaving of myth and dusty realism in which the meanderings of two Dubliners through their city on the 16th of June are recorded in the most minute detail.

The central character is Leopold Bloom, the Ulysses of the tale. (When once asked why he had made a wandering Greek the symbolic representative of Western man instead of - say - Jesus, Joyce allegedly replied that Jesus had had it easy. He had never married.) Anyway, during the course of the story Bloom meets a series of bizarre Dublin characters. In Barney Kiernan's tavern he encounters the Cyclopean figure of 'The Citizen', ' a broadshouldered deepchested stronglimbed frankeyed redhaired .. deepvoiced ruddyfaced sinewyarmed hero' who is also a bigot, a buffoon and a shameless cadger of free beer. Every bar should have one.

Joyce's last work was ' Finnegan's Wake', not a book to be read with a hangover, although reading it while drunk might help you to decode its dream - language. The hero of the book is Humphrey Chimpden Earwicker. And what is he? A publican, what else. The focus of all our waking dreams.

BALLADS

There is a great and much neglected writer who never wins literary prizes, never appears on chat shows, is honoured by no plaque or memorial statue. But this writer deserves to be counted amongst the greatest of literary drinkers. His (or her) name is Anon. Anon wrote ballads. Ballads tell of many things: wandering, war and women. But they also tell drinking tales, and ale is their inspiration.

The poet divine that cannot reach wine
Because that his money doth many times fail
Will hit on the vein to make a good strain
If he be but inspired by a pot of good ale.

One of the first English drinking songs to be printed is found in 'Gammer Gurton's Needle', a Tudor comedy. In it the singer defies the elements:

No frost nor snow, no wind I trow,
Can hurt me if I wold;
I am so wrapped, and thoroughly lapped
Of jolly good ale and old.

In a song from 'The Ipswich Minstrel' all other nourishments are spurned:

Bryng us in no bacon, for that is passing fat
But bryng us in good ale, and gyve us
i-nough of that
And bryng us in good ale.

And a seventeenth century ballad called 'In Praise of Ale' is equally vociferous in celebration of the qualities of that wonderful beverage:

All history gathers
From ancient forefathers
That Ale's the true liquor of life:
Men lived long in health
And preserved their wealth
Whilst barley-broth only was rife.

This note of chest-thrusting nationalism is not exactly unfamiliar in ballads, and it is often associated with beer drinking. A Hampshire ballad defies the French for their temerity in threatening that 'they will come and drink old England dry.' That privilege was, it seems, reserved for the heroes of English ballads. One of the foremost of these heroes was Robin Hood. In the ballad 'Robin Hood and the Pedlar' the good Robin engages in a ritual punch up with an unknown pedlar after which the gallant pair go off, quite rightly, to engage in male bonding in the nearest ale-house.

They sheathed their swords with friendly words
So merrily they did agree
They went to a tavern and there they dined
And cracked bottles most merrily.

Women also found a place in these drinking ballads. A Hampshire song, 'Three Drunken Maidens', shows women for once not as the victims of fate or rapacious men, but boozing it up with the best of them. By the end of the song they have got through 'forty pints of beer, me boys' and have drunk their maidenheads away. Probably a reasonable swap.

Being the season it is, we should mention the wassailing ballads, one of the more tolerable by-products of Christmas. These songs tend to be variations on a theme. The Gloucestershire Wassail begins:

Wassail, wassail, all over the town
Our toast it is white and our ale it is brown

and concludes by celebrating the maid:

Who tripped to the door and pulled back the pin,
For to let these jolly wassailers in.

Does one detect the faint hint of a double entendre here?

Ballads are a form of oral culture that expresses popular needs, from the celebration of 'jolly good ale' to the caustically critical portrayal of 'I'm the man, the very fat man, that waters the workers' beer'. As a literary tradition it has always stood against official culture, rather like, perhaps, the stubborn independence of small breweries in an age of multi-national corporations. A tale, then, of survival and regeneration, epitomised in one of the finest of drinking ballads, 'John Barleycorn', in which our hero is ploughed and sowed, reaped and mowed, but lived to tell the tale

For they pour him out of an old brown jug
And they call him home-brewed ale.

MORE BALLADS

Geoffrey Grigson, a poet and critic of sorts, once put together a collection of ballads. In it he claimed that after the nineteenth century the ballads of the poorer industrial communities represented a vast rubbish tip. Literary drinkers may beg to differ.

Not all ballads are about swains and swainesses leaping about in the buttercups bellowing 'Hey, nonny nonny!' before getting down to it in the long grass. Most of the best ballads of the last two centuries have grown out of urban and industrial experience. Many of these, of course, are about the great anaesthetic of the working man, drink. No communities better exemplify this rich modern tradition than those of Dublin and Newcastle. Both areas are known for their linguistic energy, their proud independence, and their fearsome thirst.

The magnificent Cameron's Strongarm is said to have originally been brewed to satisfy the considerable needs of steelworkers, and the Federation Brewery on Tyneside emerged from working men's clubs within mining communities. Interestingly, for a region which produced Andy Capp, women's drinking habits get a good airing in Tyneside ballads. Cushie Butterfield was ' a big lass and a bonny lass' who stole the heart of the songwriter less for her striking physical attributes, than for the fact that ' she likes hor beer'.

Another who liked her beer was the heroine of Tommy Armstrong's 'Wor Nanny's a Maizor' in which the eponymous Nanny is incautiously allowed into a ' pubbilic hoose' where:

'She sat and she drank till she got tight; she says "Bob, man, aa feel vary queer"
" Wey," aa sais, "thoos had nine glasses of gin, te my three gills o' beer." '

The author was no slouch in drinking matters himself. "Me dad's muse," said one of his sons, " was a mug of ale."

Stout, rather than ale, is the drink that inspires most Irish ballads, but the public bar remains the stage on which many of these dramas are played. The Dubliners came to prominence in the sixties as singers of what were called street ballads, but their subject matter tended to get off the street and into the nearest pub. In 'The Parting Glass' the singer prides himself that: 'of all the money that ever I had I spent it in good company' and bids farewell with the words: 'so lift to me the parting glass, good night and joy be with you all'. No doubt a valediction often delivered by your own local landlord.

In 'The Holy Ground' the sailors return 'to drink strong ale and porter till we make the tap room roar' and the ballad 'Preab San Ol' finishes with the defiant challenge 'another round!', a cry too often stifled in England by iniquitous licensing laws.

It is unlikely that anyone would dispute the theory that Shane MacGowan, ex-lead singer of the Pogues, is fond of a drop. In fact the songs of this remarkable Irish balladeer are drenched in the stuff. 'A Pair of brown Eyes' sets its scene:

One summer's evening drunk to hell
I sat there nearly lifeless

In 'Sally MacLennane' the narrator
'took the jeers and drank the beers and I
crawled back home at dawn
And ended up a barman in the morning'
That'll teach him.

'A Fairytale of New York' puts Christmas in its appropriate place:
'It was Christmas Eve babe
In the drunk tank
An old man said to me, won't see
another one . . .'

But just in case MacGowan's vision seems unnervingly retributive, we'll leave the last word to The Dubliners' version of 'Seven deadly Sins':
'Some say that drinking's a sin
But a gargle is fine now and then
For drinking has been in this world
For ever and ever amen .'
Amen indeed.

MALCOLM LOWRY

If readers of 'Inspire' were to embark on a literary (and drinking) pilgrimage to Cambridge they would probably wish to visit Hills Road Sixth Form College, Alma Mater to so many artistic talents. On the way they might well travel along Trumpington Road, on the corner of which lies the Leys School. The Leys spawned the original Mr Chips and, more relevantly for us, one of his pupils, Malcolm Lowry.

Lowry was brought up on the Wirral where, amongst other privations, he woke up every morning to the distant sight of the Welsh hills. One of Lowry's biographers remarked rather snootily that 'culture has never been very obtrusive on the Wirral'. Whether for this reason or for other motives of romantic rebellion Lowry, in search of experience, enlisted at the age of eighteen as a deck hand on the SS Pyrrhus. Since his wealthy middle-class family drove him to the embarkation point in the family Roller it is not wholly surprising that his fellow crew members regarded him as an object of derision. Although he was able to make merciless use of it in his fiction, his stay at sea was not altogether a happy one. It did nothing, for instance, to cure his sexual hang-ups which seemed to emanate from a complex about the size of his member and a morbid fear of syphilis. Not an ideal combination for a would-be Lothario. Still, the voyage did at least encourage a drinking habit which was soon to assume a rather significant role in his literary life. His novel 'Ultramarine' was based on his experiences at sea. Dana Hilliot, the Lowry figure, spends much of his time being abused by his shipmates, whingeing about some woman back in England and getting drunk. In one scene he meets a German minding his own business on the dockside and drags him off to the nearest bar where he immediately whacks three gins into him.

"Drei?" said the German. " All these - fur mich?"

"Ja, ja," I said. " You will be drunk."

"I was drunk when you met me."

" You will be drunker still."

"Come on now, what are you going to have now?"

"Beer. Let us get really drunk."

And so on.

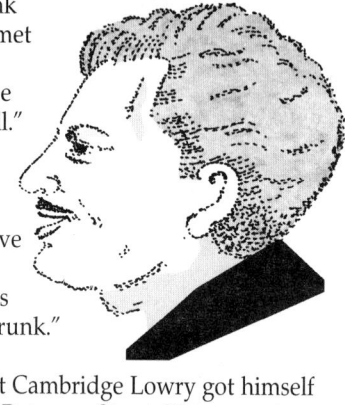

When at Cambridge Lowry got himself lodgings in Bateman Street. He was not totally happy with the place, due to his suspicion that the landlord's club foot had been caused by syphilis and that the disease might be passed on across the breakfast plates. The lodgings were, however, very close to that excellent pub, The Panton Arms. Other boozers which attracted his custom included The Maypole and The Red Cow, where he used to round off an evening's heavy drinking with exuberant bouts of fisticuffs with an obliging friend. Later he spent some time in Soho where he cultivated a reputation for eccentricity instanced by his turning up at a restaurant with a dead rabbit in a suitcase. In Granada, where it is important for a man's reputation that he should be able to hold his drink, he became known as 'el borracho ingles' and small urchins used to stone him in the street.. Lowry was never what you might call an unostentatious drinker.

Eventually he ended up in Mexico, a place that might have been waiting for him. There he discovered the subtle delights of Mexican beer, tequila and mescal, to which he gave his considerable attention. This sustained bingeing had its predictable consequences, but the efforts of a Mexican doctor to sort him out consisted of dosing him with brandy and strychnine. This didn't exactly solve the problem.

But out of Mexico with its mountains and abysses, out of Oaxaca, that city of dreadful night where Lowry was imprisoned on suspicion of being a spy, came 'Under the Volcano' one of the great novels of the twentieth century and possibly the best ever written about drinking. In it, the ex-consul Geoffrey Firmin doggedly drinks himself to death and hell. 'Under the Volcano' is about the fragility of the human soul, salvation and damnation and the redemptive power of love. Through his drunkenness the Consul seeks spiritual enlightenment (which interesting justification I offer free of charge for 'Inspire' readers' own use). Even the clouds passing above him seem to say 'Drink all morning .. drink all day. This is life.' He wonders 'what beauty can compare to that of a cantina in the early morning' but in the magnificent hell-hole that is the bar-room of the Farolito he meets his death.

Lowry himself died under uncertain circumstances at the end of a drinking bout. He is different from other literary drinkers in his treatment of drinking as something spiritual (or purgatorial). Toward the end of his life, when the writing was very much on the bar-room wall, he defiantly asserted his drinking philosophy:

' not an hour, not a moment of my drunkenness, my continual death, was not worth it : there is .. not a drink I have not made sing.'

SAMUEL BECKETT

The audience settle themselves in their seats. A dim light rises on the stage, empty but for miscellaneous rubbish. A faint cry is heard and then the light increases until full, then gradually decreases to minimum. Another faint cry is heard and then silence. The whole thing lasts perhaps 35 seconds.

That was 'Breath', a play by the Irish dramatist Samuel Beckett, first produced in Britain in 1969. Not an obvious rival to 'The Mousetrap', perhaps. Understandably, Beckett's early plays met a mixed reaction from the theatre-going public, but their stock rose rapidly, apparently proving particularly popular amongst Scottish librarians.

Beckett was a close friend of James Joyce (q.v.), another exiled Irish writer, but their literary worlds were markedly dissimilar. Joyce spilled thousands of words celebrating and affirming the many varieties of the human spirit; Beckett devoted his time and energy to exploring its absurdity and futility.

The birth of Beckett's characters tends to be the death of them, or as Pozzo says in 'Waiting for Godot': 'one day we were born, one day we shall die, the same day, the same second .. They give birth astride of a grave, the light gleams an instant, then it's night once more.' The creatures of Beckett's fiction are usually old, miserable and ill. They spend their time hobbling without any obvious purpose from one place to another, talking obsessively about disease, despair and death.

At first sight, then, Beckett's world would seem to be far removed from that of the social drinker. Quite the contrary, in fact. There is a popular misconception that pubs are places of light, merriment, music and constant cheerful badinage. If they were, of course, no sensible person would go anywhere near them. Most good pubs are dark, murky places where drinking men and women can if they choose, find a dusty corner where they may sit and soak and peacefully fester to their soul's content. Hence, no doubt, the fascination which pubs exercised over Beckett's imagination.

He apparently didn't drink much as a student, but after he had moved to France in the 1920's he made up for lost time. His amateur rugby career was handicapped by his tendency to celebrate before the game, and at the end of one particularly effervescent celebratory dinner with Joyce and other assorted literati the young Beckett found himself abandoned by his exasperated friends in a heap and a urinal.

On his periodic visits to Ireland he indulged in bouts of serious drinking in out-of-the-way pubs where he would scribble off rambling notes such as: 'I am deteriorating now very rapidly. An insensible mass of alcohol, nicotine and feminine intoxication. A heap of guts.' He would then send the notes to his friends. After one such session he arrived home without his keys and adopted the imaginative tactic of trying to batter down the back door with his head. It didn't work. Like Joyce, his relationship with his mother country was ambiguous. He once wearily described Dublin Sundays as 'mist and rain and chimes and teetotal'.

As befitted a man who was so deeply immersed in the world of his imagination, Beckett was often a solo drinker. He particularly drank alone when things were going badly for him creatively, 'going on the blind' as he put it. Many of the characters in his plays and novels are determinedly solitary creatures. Winnie, in 'Happy Days' muses: 'Ah yes, if only I could bear to be alone, I mean prattle away with not a soul to hear'. Winnie, it should be pointed out, is at the time buried up to her waist in earth, which may have influenced her views somewhat.

If Beckett's stories present a remorselessly bleak world, they are also often richly comic in effect, and his friends have attested that the author himself could be an amusing and convivial drinking companion. One of his mistresses claimed that he only unravelled himself after copious amounts of alcohol: a clear hint to any amorous young woman having trouble with a bashful suitor. He took an active part in the rehearsals of his plays, and these sessions used to involve some fairly concentrated boozing in bars such as Mooney's pub in London. The Irish actors, Patrick Magee and Jack MacGowran, appeared in several productions of his plays, and both being fierce drinkers in their own right, were able to offer their valuable support during these important off-stage activities.

In his later years, when old and suffering from ill-health, he continued to take his daily lunchtime beer and pursue his solitary working existence. Like his fictional creations, Beckett clung to life against the odds. His most famous play is 'Waiting for Godot', in which two rather desolate characters wait for someone who never turns up. The play acts as a metaphor for the absurdities, frustrations and contradictions of our lives, exemplified by the final lines, where the two central protagonists demonstrate the well-worn tactics of stubborn customers at closing time:

'VLADIMIR: Well? Shall we go?
ESTRAGON: Yes, let's go.
They do not move.'

DR. JOHNSON

Engraved on a thousand artificial beams above a thousand artificial bars are the following words:

'there is nothing which has yet been contrived by man, by which so much happiness is produced as by a good tavern or inn.'

The problem is, of course, that the pub in which this piece of wisdom is displayed is frequently so dire as to provide its own contradiction. Nevertheless, it's worth exploring the rest of the text from which the above quotation is an extract.

'. . at a tavern there is a general freedom from anxiety. (Hm. Not if you're straining your lungs trying to attract the attention of the living dead painting their nails behind the bar.) You are sure you are welcome: and the more noise you make, the more trouble you give, the more good things you call for, the welcomer you are. (Hm, again. Far more likely, in my experience, that your friendly host will bar you for life.)

Several contradictions here, then, and the author of the above lines, Samuel Johnson, was himself a man of many contradictions. He was and is a writer more famous for being a writer than for anything he wrote. He was known for the elegance of his prose and for the grotesque disorder of his physical appearance. He preached the necessity of good manners while his eating habits were, well - interesting:

'When at table he was totally absorbed . . . his looks seemed riveted to his plate . . his appetite . . was so fierce and indulged with such intenseness, that while in the act of eating, the veins of his forehead swelled, and generally a strong perspiration was visible.'

He mocked Scotsmen, but befriended a Scot, James Boswell, from whose biography of Johnson the quotation above is taken. He trumpeted the virtues of drinking water, but spent a considerable amount of his life in inns. When he did settle down to something approximating to domestic life, it was under the roof of a certain Henry Thale whose occupation was, appropriately, a brewer. Johnson lived in an age when life was lived publicly and to excess. Boswell said that Johnson 'was not a temperate man either in eating or drinking. He could refrain, but he could not use moderately.' The battle-cry of the binge drinker. Certainly Boswell was well qualified to judge. According to his own writings, when not fawning obsequiously on Johnson, he seems to have divided his time between drinking himself into a stupor, fornicating energetically with whores, collapsing into paroxysms of guilt and remorse, and then re-embarking on the whole process with undiminished enthusiasm.

Johnson built his fame on being a man of many parts. At one stage in his life he made the tactical error of embarking on the teaching profession. Born too early to model his teaching methods on the admirable Mr. Creakle in 'David Copperfield', he found himself unable to keep the little swine in his charge in order and abandoned the whole nasty business. He was, in any case and like many literary drinkers, a natural melancholic. He once made the mistake of falling in love - with a woman described by Macaulay as being ' short, fat, coarse and . . . painted half an inch thick', presumably implying some form of criticism. Macaulay put Johnson's infatuation down to his poor eyesight. Either way it may not have increased his chances of shaking off his characteristic gloom. When asked if a man was ever truly happy, he replied: 'Never, but when he is drunk.'

He suffered great poverty in his early life when his regular diet consisted of 'a sixpennyworth of veal and a pennyworth of bread' in an alehouse near Drury Lane. This must have been a considerable privation for a man of whom it was said: 'the sight of food affected him as it affects wild beasts and birds of prey'. His fame, however, once gained, has endured. Johnson has become something of an institution, and like many institutions has come in for his fair share of mockery. A recent television production of 'Vanity Fair' began with the iconoclastic Becky Sharp hurling a copy of Johnson's dictionary out of a carriage window. Robbie Coltrane enjoyed himself as a particularly buffoonish Johnson in an episode of 'Blackadder'.

Literary drinkers owe him a debt, nevertheless. He is one of the great celebrants of the English public house. Boswell records how Johnson 'expatiated on the felicity of England in its taverns and inns, and triumphed over the French for not having, in any perfection, the tavern life.' And if the literary drinkers' pilgrimage takes them in search of Johnson, they might do worse than head for the heart of the City of London, to pub full of murky nooks and alcoves beloved of literary drinkers, a pub where - incredibly - a pint of excellent real ale can be had for just over £1.50, Johnson's pub: The Cheshire Cheese.

ROBERT LOUIS STEVENSON

Edinburgh is a treasure island for literary drinkers. There is, for instance, The Oxford Bar in Young Street where it is said that every Scottish writer of the twentieth century has ended up sooner or later. I can attest to its qualities, not the least of which is the occasional guest appearance of megalithic Scottish front row forwards with a propensity for regaling their fellow drinkers from the top of a stepladder.

There is also Rutherford's Bar in Drummond Street, described in one CAMRA guide as being 'vibrant' and 'splendid'. It was once the favourite howff (magnificently evocative word) of Robert Louis Stevenson. Stevenson spent much of his time as a student in tireless tours of the brothels and low-life pubs of the Edinburgh Old Town, often in the company of his heavy drinking buddies, Charles Baxter and James Ferrier. The latter's later alcoholism was laid by his mother at Stevenson's door. Rather harsh, but Stevenson's life at the time was certainly neither to the liking of his father or the good citizens of Calvinist Edinburgh, of whom Stevenson wrote:

'O fine religious, decent folk
In virtues flaunting gold and scarlet
I sneer between two puffs of smoke
Give me the publican and harlot.'

One publican who made his mark on the young Stevenson was Brash of Lothian Road, a gentleman of flamboyantly foul moods and manners, Since Stevenson spent as much time and as little money in his pubs as he could, perhaps Brash may be excused. At any rate Stevenson immortalised him in 'Brasheanna', a sonnet in which the good publican is imagined after death in the fiery pit, where, acting to the last in the grand manner of his fellow professionals:

'he doles
Damned liquors out to hellward-faring souls
And as his impotent anger ranges high
Gibbers and gurgles at the shades of men.'

Such carefree days were not to last for long, however. Stevenson got married. His association with women had often not been a happy one. His nurse, Alison Cunningham, was a religious maniac. Her predecessor had been discovered in a gin palace with the child left rather unsportingly outside. Having spent his youth in fruitless pursuit of a woman called Fanny Sitwell, he transferred his affections to another Fanny, a Mrs Osbourne who some consider to have been one of the great harridans of literary legend. Not content with burning the manuscripts of which she disapproved, she seems to have spent her inexhaustible energies in driving off Stevenson's old drinking companions. 'What,' wrote Stevenson in a plaintive letter to Baxter, 'would I not give to steal this evening with you .. away to dear Brash's, now defunct!'

Despite such privations, Stevenson continued to celebrate the drinking world in his verse and prose. In a poem called 'Heather Ale', the Pictish people hold the secret of an ale 'sweeter far than honey (and) stronger far than wine'. A tyrannical king tries to force the last Picts to divulge the secret, but they honourably choose death instead:

'in vain is the torture
Fire shall never avail
Here dies in my bosom
The secret of Heather Ale.'

'The Bottle Ale' is another tale about damnation and drink in which a bottle with a curse on it eventually ends up in the hands of a boatswain who is happy to risk hell for a life that promises endless supplies of booze. But if any book offers a glimpse into a drinker's soul it is 'Dr Jekyll and Mr Hyde', surely one of the most magnificent insights into the drinking condition ever written. Consider the following as a depiction of that uplifting of the spirit occasioned by the first thirsted-for drink at the end of the working week:

'I came to myself as out of a great sickness.. I felt younger, lighter, happier in body . . conscious of a heady recklessness . . my devil had been long caged, he came out roaring.'

And how about this as an insight into those Sunday mornings when you wake up with a very indistinct memory of how you did not get home the previous night :

'I looked down; my clothes hung formlessly on my shrunken limbs; the hand that lay on my knee was corded and hairy.'

Interestingly, Jekyll, when Hyde, holes up in Soho. There, cornered, he transfers himself back to Jekyll by drinking what Stevenson, in his last gift to us, presumably intended as a warning against nitrokeg:

'He put the glass to his lips and drank at one gulp. A cry followed; he reeled, staggered, clutched at the table and held on . . . . his face became suddenly black - '

Horrible.

KENNETH GRAHAME

It may seem rather harsh to drag Kenneth Grahame onto our list of literary drinkers. He was quite a shy and retiring man by all accounts, and it's hard to imagine him knocking them back with some of the professional boozers who have graced our earlier editions. In addition, his early experiences of drinking men were not altogether positive. His father had compensated for an uncongenial legal career by giving the bottle some serious attention, with results that were not to his professional advantage.

Kenneth Grahame's own life was not without its vicissitudes. After a childhood that he later looked back on as idyllic, he was plunged into the world of city banking. Searching for some sort of literary career, he encountered the grisly bunch of end-of-century aesthetes who infested the end of the 19th Century and were probably indirectly responsible for the First World War. Unsurprisingly, Grahame was unnerved by their absinthe-fuelled excesses, but was himself given to ludicrous burblings about goat-footed Pan and such like. Then (to cap it all) he got married. When you discover that his correspondence with his fiancee was peppered with such toe-curling sentiments as ' so glad you're corled "Elspeth", nannie, coz I didn't no it & I like it so much' it comes as no surprise to find that the more intimate grapplings of married life came as something of a shock to them both.

All in all it's understandable that Grahame sought solace in the rural fantasies which ultimately engendered 'The Wind in the Willows'.

The book has been firmly stuck in the category labelled 'children's literature', but this may do it a disservice. Rat, Mole and Badger, for instance, like some Edwardian understudies for 'Last of the Summer Wine', go trolling off in search of adventures, which quite rightly and quite often seem to involve drink. When Ratty entertains a travelling Sea Rat, he produces a ' long-necked straw-covered flask containing bottled sunshine'. When the magnificent Toad, who if he were alive today would surely be the Conservative candidate for Lord Mayor of London, escapes from captivity, the first place he heads for is The Red Lion. Mole's house boasts a 'skittle alley, with benches along it and little wooden tables marked with rings that hinted at beer mugs'. When the rat visits, he compliments Mole on his discrimination as a beer drinker: 'The rat was busy examining the label on one of the beer bottles. "I perceive this to be Old Burton," he remarked approvingly. " Sensible Mole! The very thing! Now we shall be able to mull some ale!" ' And they proceed to get some field mice blotto, and quite right too.

The appearance of beer in 'The Wind in the Willows' is not surprising. For Kenneth Grahame the golden age of English pastoral was inseparable from English ale and English pubs. In an earlier piece called 'Loafing' he describes the Loafer, prone on his back gazing at the sky, before being:

' called back to earth by. . . a gradual, consuming, Pantagruelian, god-like thirst : a thirst to thank Heaven on. So, with a sigh half of regret, half of anticipation, he bends his solitary steps towards the nearest inn. Tobacco for one is good; to commune with oneself and be still is truest wisdom; but beer is a thing of deity - beer is divine.' Hear! Hear!

Another hymn of praise to beer occurs in 'A Woodland at Home' where Grahame describes a copse as ' a little heaven of shade, stored with everything a sensible man can ask on a tropical day: everything, that is, but beer . . .' In a piece called 'On The High Road ' (perhaps he was a rather strait-laced ancestor of Kerouac) Grahame reaches at last his 'destined rustic inn. There, in its homely, comfortable strangeness, after unnumbered chops with country ale, the hard facts of life begin to swim in a golden mist.' The country ale must have had quite a kick, because within a few sentences the traveller comes to the conclusion that : 'This is undoubtedly the best and greatest country in the world; and none but good fellows abide in it'.

A friend of mine, much given to political incorrectness, used to describe himself after a drinking bout as having been 'gassed as a badger'. While the Badger of 'The Wind in the Willows' is a somewhat sober citizen, the same cannot be said for the story's other strangely humanoid creatures. And if you want further proof, look about you as you sit on your bar stool. There in the corner is Rat, doing the crossword. Beside him fusses the Mole, cleaning and tidying beermats. And that flash and obnoxious plonker at the bar, boring everyone brainless with his endless and tedious opinions - that's the Toad.

P. G. WODEHOUSE

The history of English Literature is studded with examples of writers for whom good drink and good drinking were the elixir of creative life. Nor were these scribblers necessarily tortured souls, wrestling with their inner demons in some shadowy and poverty-stricken attic. The whole point about drinking, after all, is that it is meant to be fun. So, it seems, thought P.G.Wodehouse.

If for no other reason, Wodehouse would be assured of an honoured place in the ranks of literary drinkers on account of his gleeful compilation of terms for that blissful condition of being 'merry'. In no particular order, try these, all taken from his novels and short stories: boiled, awash, stinko, tanked, tight as an owl, under the sauce, ossified, fried to the tonsils, scrooched, whiffled and woozled.

Although a series of financial and political intrusions into his life kept Wodehouse abroad for long periods, the world of his imagination remained rooted in the country of his birth. Wodehouse's fiction is full of inspirational names of English villages: Twing, Old Crockford, Market Snodsbury, Lower-Smattering-on-the Wold. And in these villages, of course, lie English inns: The Bull and Bush, The Beetle and Wedge, The Goose and Gherkin, The Goose and Grasshopper, The Stitch in Time.

Perhaps the most famous of Wodehouse's parade of English inns is the Angler's Rest where the benign and philosophic Mr Mulliner holds forth to his (fairly) captive nightly audience. The pub is, as pubs should be, an English idyll: 'Twilight had fallen on the little garden of the Angler's Rest, and the air was fragrant with the sweet smell of jasmine and tobacco plant. Stars were peeping out. Blackbirds sang drowsily in the shrubbery. . It was, in short, as a customer who had looked in for a gin and tonic rather happily put it, a nice evening'. The Angler's Rest is frequented by regulars identified only by their chosen tipple: 'a Stout and Mild', 'A Whisky and Splash', 'A Small Bass'. Serving this mixed assortment is the quintessential barmaid, Miss Postlethwaite, in whom 'the quiet splendour of her costume and the devout manner in which she pulled the beer handle told their own story.' Indeed.

Wodehouse, quite rightly, was fond of old men who liked their drink. Galahad (Gally) Threepwood 'had discovered the prime grand secret of eternal youth .. plenty of alcohol and a lifelong belief that it was bad form to go to bed before three in the morning'. Galahad had firm views about the road to good health: 'No healthy person really needs food. If people would only stick to drinking, doctors would go out of business.'

Villains are never really villainous in the world of Wodehouse, but those who come close can easily be identified by their lifestyle choices. Sir Gregory Parsloe, who pits himself against Galahad in 'Pigs Have Wings' loses any sympathy from the reader when he bans his pigman, George Cyril Wellbeloved, from the solace of an after-work beer. 'What beats me,' says the foolish Sir Gregory, 'is why you fellers want to go about swilling and soaking. Look at me .I never touch the stuff.' Hubris brings its inevitable punishment, however, and after a broken romance Sir Gregory is brought to understand the error of his ways. 'A tankard stood beside him . .. , and in the manner in which he raised it to his lips there was something gay and swashbuckling. A woman is only a woman, he seemed to be saying, but a frothing pint is a drink.'

Romance, of course, lies at the heart of the Wodehouse comic world and even, or especially, here beer plays its supportive part. Malevolent aunts who put obstacles in the way of young lovers are characterised by their vicious prejudices: 'Lady Hermione shuddered. She was not a woman who had ever been fond of public houses.' The inestimable qualities of the young romantic heroines, however, are revealed to us through appropriately alcoholic imagery. ' "Oh, Bertie," she said, in a voice like beer trickling out of a jug.'

Even hangovers are brought into service as a means whereby Wodehousian good can be distilled from suffering. It is after Jeeves produces a miracle tissue restorer that Bertie Wooster makes the life-changing decision to employ him. The wonderfully named Oofy Prosser is dissuaded from an unsuitable romantic alliance by awakening from a refreshing sleep on the hearth-rug and beholding the frightening visage of Algernon Aubrey, the infant son of Bingo Little.

Equally surprisingly, the image of enforced abstinence teaches its own lesson in the world of Wodehouse. When Wodehouse's young heroes suffer, they suffer in terms that only literary drinkers can fully understand. 'Freddie experienced the sort of abysmal soul sadness which afflicts one of Tolstoi's Russian peasants when, after putting in a heavy day's work strangling his father, beating his wife, and dropping the baby into the city reservoir, he turns to the cupboard, only to find the vodka-bottle empty.'

JOHN CLARE

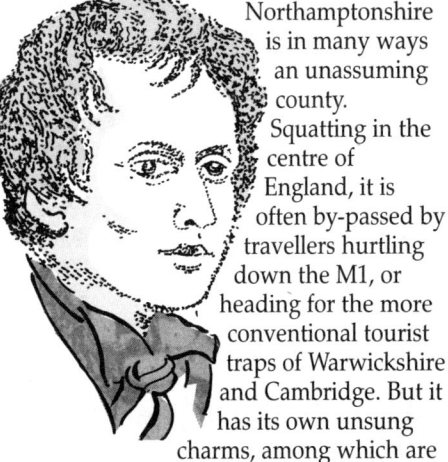

Northamptonshire is in many ways an unassuming county. Squatting in the centre of England, it is often by-passed by travellers hurtling down the M1, or heading for the more conventional tourist traps of Warwickshire and Cambridge. But it has its own unsung charms, among which are some admirable villages hosting equally admirable pubs. It was in the then Northamptonshire village of Helpston, in 1793, that the poet John Clare was born. Helpston has now been claimed, or swallowed up, by an expanded Cambridgeshire, but Northamptonshire folk quite rightly continue to claim Clare as their own.

Literary drinkers can make their own pilgrimage, if they wish, to the present day Helpston, and celebrate John Clare's life and work during an annual festival held around the Blue Bell pub, a most appropriate site for a poet whose very sensible appreciation of women, song and beer makes it rather ironic that he is best known for his later descent into madness.

Clare's father arrived in Helpston some thirty years before the poet's birth. He was a big, swaggering fellow, and his capacity to drink a gallon of beer at a sitting clearly made him ideally qualified for the post of village schoolmaster, a post which he occupied until having seduced Clare's mother he vanished as suddenly as he had arrived.

His son evinced an early taste for ale in a Stamford pub called The Hole in the Wall. Throughout his life, Clare demonstrated a further taste and talent for beer-drinking ballads; one of these, 'The Toper's Rant', rightly proclaims that it is the duty of every patriotic English man or woman to drink as much good beer as possible:

'Give me an old crone of a fellow
Who loves to drink ale in a horn
And sing racy songs when he's mellow
Which topers sung ere he was born'

The dictionary definition of a 'toper', readers may be interested to know, is one who ' drinks intoxicating liquor to excess, especially habitually'. Here's to a good tope, say I.

Clare's publishers seem to have failed to see things in quite the same grown-up way. One described him in a letter as 'a fiddler- loves ale- likes the girls- somewhat idle – hates work.' Thinly disguised envy, one presumes. Clare was a great admirer of another so-called 'peasant poet', Robert Burns, celebrated in an earlier article in this series. One of Clare's later ballads is written in Burns' style, and in praise of ale. It appears from the poem that Clare was in the habit of drinking strong nut-brown ale by the quart. Perhaps, under these circumstances, it's not altogether surprising that Clare's publisher later extracted a promise from the poet to keep sober for a year.

He didn't always stick to it, though. A later letter confesses that he 'went a frolicking yesterday . . got too much of Barleycorn broth . . fell down and got a black eye.' A late publisher bewailed Clare's tendency to become 'a little too elated with a glass of ale if you indulged him in it', and the onset of Clare's later bouts of depression was marked by the poet's account of himself as reduced to 'small beer's sad reality'.

Although Clare was in many ways forced to accede to the demands and opinions of editors and aristocratic patrons, he never lost his strong sense of social injustice. This emerges most powerfully in his poem 'The Parish', not published because of its radical views until after his death. The poem contains a series of biting satirical portraits of representative social types, where pride and hypocrisy sit side by side, often revealed through drinking metaphors. 'Young Brag''s affectation and posturing is reflected in his drinking habits; ' sips his wine in fashionable pride/ And thrusts in scorn the homely ale aside'. In contrast, the honest and unassuming local vicar is apotheosised through his hospitality offered to 'plain old farmers' who came to 'taste his ale'.

In later life, now sadly resident in an asylum, Clare took commissions for poems in exchange for beer. This allowed him on some occasions to celebrate to such an extent in the local town that the authorities found themselves obliged to limit the extent of his liberty.

Clare died in 1864. His body was returned to Helpston, where – very appropriately - the coffin spent its last night above ground in a local pub, the Exeter Arms. Clare's reputation has continued to grow since his death. He is a genuine poet of the people, and a representative of a real 'Middle England', far more worthy than the distorted versions offered by certain national daily newspapers.

CHARLES BUKOWSKI

Time to throw off all restraint. Time to abandon the pretence that 'literary drinkers' retain a precarious but productive balance between Apollonian artistic creation and Dionysiac alcoholic indulgence. Welcome to Charles Bukowski.

Somebody somewhere once hypothesised that by the age of fifty every man gains the face he deserves. A rotten trick on the part of fate, I've always thought. In support of the theory, however, there is always Bukowski's face. A monument of Michelangelo-esque proportions to the drinking life. A Matterhorn of crevices and crags, of scars and swollen veins, studded with two eyes that look like what's left at the bottom of the glass by the side of the bed on the morning after the proverbial night before.

Rather surprisingly, Bukowski did manage to interrupt his heroic drinking bouts sufficiently often to get a few things down on paper. His most loyal disciple would be hard pressed to dispute that some of his poetry is fairly grisly doggerel, but amongst the dross there are some marvellously disillusioned gems of insights into twentieth century American life. In 'Post Office' the central character, Henry Chinaski, escapes from the banality of the American Dream by immersing himself in a world of one night stands, racetracks, and – gloriously – beer. Henry Chinaski resurfaces in 'Barfly', a film starring Mickey O'Rourke which celebrates, if that's the word, Bukowski's drinking life. He is described as a man 'who drinks because there is nothing else to do'. In a neat inversion of Hollywood romance he meets a woman 'even more alcoholic' than he is. She drinks 'because it is the only thing to do'. Logical. Theirs is not exactly a conventional affair. " I've got to tell you," she says, "if some man came by with a fifth of whiskey I'm afraid I'd go with him." Logical again.

The bar they drink in, 'The Golden Horn', is light years away from the saccharine nonsense of the bar in 'Cheers'. Here Eddie the bartender and Chinaski engage in regular and brutal fistfights for no other reason than because they can. The bar is also inhabited by a grisly collection of lost souls such as Lilly who is described as tedium personified: 'even when a draft beer is put in front of her it loses its good beerishness and becomes a flat yellow substance'. 'Inspire' readers may recognise the type from within the circle of their own drinking acquaintances.

Bukowski's writing was always resolutely anti-heroic. Fairly typical is the beginning of his short story entitled 'The Life of a Bum' : 'Harry awakened in his bed, hungover. Badly hungover.' In his famous collection of short stories 'Hot Water Music' he muses on the life of a literary drinker and doesn't find it a condition much worth celebrating: 'That was the trouble with being a writer, that was the main trouble – leisure time, excessive leisure time. You had to wait around for the buildup until you could write and while you were waiting you went crazy, and while you were going crazy you drank and the more you drank the crazier you got. There was nothing glorious about the life of a writer or the life of a drinker.'

But Bukowski's work is, despite all this, not defeatist. In another short story, 'Beer at the Corner Bar' the narrator explains that: 'after a lifetime spent in bars I had entirely lost my feeling for them'. Obviously, therefore, he goes into another one. There he meets the bar bore to end all bar bores who without warning turns confrontational and orchestrates a chorus of abuse from the rest of the customers directed at our narrator. Calmly, he sits out the abuse, finishes his (several) beers and then, as with so many Bukowski characters, simply survives.

'I got up slowly and walked out. Nobody followed me. I walked up the boulevard, found my street. . . I opened my door and walked in. There was one beer in the refrigerator. I opened it and drank it.' In such small ways are our victories over life signalled.

PIVO

There is a postcard on sale in Prague which is basically made up of the word 'Pivo' repeated endlessly across the page. Quite right too, for 'pivo' is Czech for 'beer', and beer, as countless pilgrims will attest, is what Czechoslovakia is about. Since the Czechs are also rightly proud of their writers - remember they had the taste to elect a playwright as their political leader instead of a lawyer or a failed bus conductor - it is time to pay an overdue visit to the literary drinkers of Prague. Na zdravi !

No reasonable person could doubt Czech drinking credentials. Apart from anything else, they have some admirable drinking customs which English publicans would do well to note. One custom says that you should never under any circumstances use the same glass when changing one kind of brew for another. Another says that the obligatory toast (see above) is only valid if everyone on your table takes it up and then slams the glass on the table. Breaks the ice at parties.

History is kind to Czech drinkers. The first Czech king, Vratislav, had the imaginative idea of decreeing that his taxes should be paid in hops. King Wenceslas, despite popular legend, didn't waste his time trudging through snow after wood-thieving peasants, but occupied himself far more usefully by rescinding an order prohibiting brewing which had been decreed by some godless bishop. He went further and passed a law prohibiting the export of Bohemian hops, quite rightly invoking the death penalty as the ultimate deterrent.

His modern descendants keep up the good work. Czech drinkers are thought to drink more beer per capita than any other people.

The average Czech puts away well over 300 pints each year. The real pivnice habitue will leave such a modest total well behind. Where British workers will gulp down early morning watery coffee, and the French risk a tentative cognac, the Czech working man can be found sitting contentedly outside a bar heaving down a few pints of his breakfast beer.

As long as you have the sense to flee the horrors of the tourist-ridden Karlova, a tour of Prague bars will bring a series of bibulous and bibliophilic delights. If you first stoke yourself up with the richly satisfying triumvirate of vepro, knedlo and zelo (pork, dumplings and cabbage) you will be ready to give due attention to such beery treasures as Krusovice, Radegast, Gambrinus and Staropramen, the pride of Prague. And if you choose your bars carefully you will also tread in the footsteps of a series of Czech writers whose works give appropriate prominence to the art and science of beer drinking.

The Konvikt Pub in Konviktska is not a bad place to start if you want to rub shoulders with hard drinking local literary aspirants and launch into Cambrinus Plzen. A tramp across the Vltava river will get you to U Kocouva in Nerudova, under the shadow of the Hrad, 'that unbroken sheer blank wall ' of Prague Castle, as described by the famous beer drinking English writer Hilaire Belloc. It is a good murky, smoky bar, if apt to be infested by local painters trying to flog you their appalling etchings. It is certainly not difficult to see how from places such as these Kafka's heroes might have struggled out to make their hopeless journeys along the maze of streets that climb towards the castle.

The most famous drinking figure in Czech fiction is probably Jaroslav Hasek's Svejk, another in the long literary list of unassuming rogues who manage to survive the malevolent attentions of the egomaniac forces of church and state. Svejk's main aims in life are to keep alive and find a decent bar, not necessarily in that order of priority.

He begins his adventures just before the start of the First World War in a pub called The Chalice, having ' a dark black beer', and manages to get himself and the landlord arrested for treason. The Chalice, or the U Kalicha in its Czech version, has unfortunately become a tourist fly-trap, which must be whirling the good soldier about in his grave. On the other hand, he'd probably see the joke.

A literary bar that has so far survived the excesses of tourism, largely by dint of keeping the buggers out, is the magnificent U Zlateho Tygra, The Golden Tiger, a dispenser of some memorable pilsner and the erstwhile haunt of Bohumil Hrabal, the author of 'I Served the King of England' and 'Closely Observed Trains'. The former book tells of the adventures of Ditie, a boy in the catering and licensing trade, who survives by the usual barman's tactic of declaring undying friendship to anyone with money in their hand. Hrabal had his own reserved seat in the Tygra where he held court daily to a string of visitors, including once, in a moment of impressive discernment, Bill Clinton. In his life and in his works, Hrabal gave testimony to that wisest of Czech proverbs, ' Wherever beer is brewed, all is well.'

JACK LONDON

In the famous drinking ballad, 'John Barleycorn', the crop, 'pale and wan' in the midsummer sun, is miraculously transformed into 'homebrewed ale'. Burns also used the term as a personification for ale in his poem 'Tam o' Shanter:

Inspiring, bold John Barleycorn!
What dangers thou can make us scorn!
Wi tippenny (ale) we fear nae evil;

It seems a long way from fields of British barley to the bitter wastes of the Klondike and the Yukon. But it was in these wintry territories that Jack London, the author of 'John Barleycorn: Alcoholic Memories' made his literary name.

London is best known for such tales as 'The Call of the Wild' and 'White Fang': stories that explore the primordial natural forces within men, beasts and the savage environment where they live and die. In 'John Barleycorn' he explored a different, but equally bleak world, 'frozen as absolute zero', the world of the alcoholic.

During one of his harbour-side drinking bouts he found himself leaning against the bar with Young Nelson, king of the oyster pirates, whose very reasonable whim it was 'to drink beer, and to have me drink beer with him.' London was at that time relatively inexperienced in the etiquette of drinking and after some time the blinding revelation came to him that there was a reason that the older man kept buying the beer. 'I had let him buy six drinks and never once offered to treat.' London had failed to buy his round. Quite rightly ashamed of his appalling dereliction of drinking duty, he went on a wild bender in which he seems to have bought drinks for half the harbour-side and predictably ended up stony broke. Perhaps this early correlation between drink and shame was the precursor for the very negative feelings about drink which emerge in his autobiographical writings. John Barleycorn becomes a character in the book of that name, and London's musings on that personification lead him to such cheery observations as 'I know that within this disintegrating body .. I carry a skeleton' and frequently broods on the relationship between John Barleycorn and what he calls 'the Noseless One'. In another bout of alcohol-induced depression he claimed to an unfortunate drinking companion that after a couple or more drinks he should begin to feel 'the white worm tunnelling through our brains'. Surprisingly, under the circumstances, they ordered another round.

On another occasion, well tanked up, he fell overboard and the sensation of finding himself floating in the biggest vat in the world led him to seductive thoughts of easy suicide. Interestingly, the same impulse brings about the death of the eponymous hero of London's novel 'Martin Eden'.

So far so bad, then. But this is not, predictably, the whole story. Throughout his writings, London can't help but celebrate the connection between good drink and good fellowship. 'Heaven forfend me' he says 'from (men) cold of heart and cold of head who don't smoke, drink or swear'. And apparently, 'The brightest spots in my child life were the saloons'. This early revelation was later reinforced: 'In the saloons life was different. Men talked with great voices, laughed great laughs, and there was an atmosphere of greatness.' London even went so far as to claim that 'saloon-keepers are notoriously good fellows.' He boasts of vanquishing a group of students in a 'beer bust' during which he reflected that he had not drunk steam beer for years, but 'when I had I had drunk with men, and I guessed I could show these youngsters some ability in beer guzzling'. And he did.

Fame did not always bring him happiness.

He is said to have sacked a servant who was presumptuous enough to say to him, 'Will God have some beer?' but he did at least spend his last days in that part of California famed for its wine grapes. Jack London lived for conflict. In that perhaps lies his oddly confrontational attitude to the drinking and literary drinking that so defined his life.

THOMAS HARDY

The conscientious student of past copies of 'The Good Beer Guide' will know that in Dorchester in Dorset there was a brewery that was itself a tribute to the latest in our list of literary drinkers, Thomas Hardy. In fact, on the desk in front of me is a small bottle, numbered P17727, of Thomas Hardy's Ale, brewed in 1987 by Eldridge Pope. It claims to be the strongest beer in Britain and to mature in the bottle over at least 25 years. I must get round to drinking it soon.

Hardy was a friend of the then director of Eldridge Pope, so it is perhaps not surprising that his novels have much to say about beer and cider drinking. In a letter to a fellow writer, Hardy admitted that he had 'never found alcohol helpful to novel writing in any degree'. This is not the same thing, of course, as failing to appreciate its other virtues. Robert Graves, in 'Goodbye to All That' describes how during a visit to Hardy, the writer 'grew enthusiastic in praise of cyder, which he had drunk since a boy, as the finest medicine he knew.'

Hardy's poem 'Great Things', a lyrical celebration of what makes life worth living, appropriately begins with cider:

Sweet cyder is a great thing,
A great thing to me'
Spinning down to Weymouth town
By Ridgeway thirstily

It is perhaps sadly appropriate that some of the beers named after Hardy no longer exist, since Hardy himself was a chronicler of cultures and societies teetering on the cliff edge of the past.

Some critics have argued that the world of Hardy's novels steadily darkened during his writing career. It could also be argued, interestingly, that the part that drinking plays in the novels also becomes increasingly sombre.

Writers like Flora Thompson (Lark Rise to Candleford) have attested to the significance that the drinking of ale had in agricultural communities, where long hard days in the fields created gargantuan thirsts. Then, as now, pubs also lay at the heart of the village community. In 'Far from the Madding Crowd', Warren's Malthouse provides an important social centre for the villagers, where they drink warmed cider from the 'God-Forgive-Me', a two-handled tall mug, so named 'because its size makes any given toper feel ashamed of himself when he sees its bottom in drinking it empty'. Later in the novel, with unfortunate consequences, Joseph Poorgrass, while on an important errand, is seduced by the charms of 'the old inn Buck's Head'. There he finds the familiar encouragement of fellow drinkers: 'drink, Joseph, and don't restrain yourself', and is offered the unassailable argument that ' after all, many people haven't the gift of enjoying a wet, and since we be highly favoured with a power that way, we should make the most o't'.

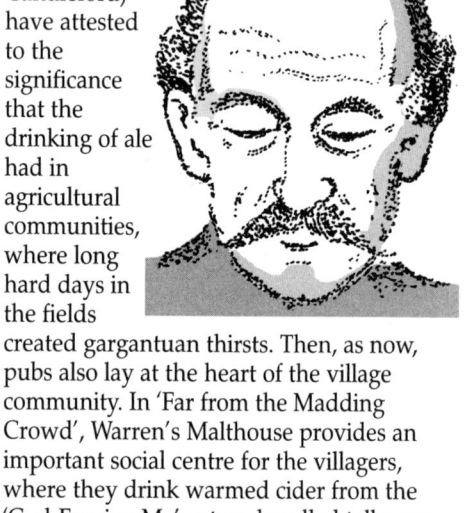

In 'Tess of the d'Urbervilles', however, the heroine's long downfall begins when her father, bursting with pride at his newly discovered knightly lineage, gets aristocratically plastered at Rolliver's Inn.

Michael Henchard, the tragic hero of 'The Mayor of Casterbridge' finds himself at the beginning of the novel in a refreshment tent at a village fair. He foolishly allows his wife to turn him from a tent which sells 'Good Home-brewed Ale and Cyder' to a 'furmity booth'. Here he mixes the horrible stuff with rum and having passed through the usual stages of drunkenness proceeds to sell off his wife and daughter to the highest bidder. Rather an excessive punishment, one feels.

Finally, the grim tale of Jude Fawley, in 'Jude the Obscure' is not much lightened by the central character's involvement with strong drink. At an early stage, he is seduced by the manipulative Arabella, the barmaid of The Lamb and Flag. Jude's comparative innocence at that stage of his career may be judged by his remark that 'somehow it seems odd to come to a public house for beer on a Sunday evening'. With such an attitude his eventual entrapment comes as no surprise.

But to return on a more positive note to the excellent bottle of Thomas Hardy's Ale, which I really must open before long: on the bottle is a quotation from Hardy's 'The Trumpet Major'. It describes Dorchester's strong beer, and may be taken as a conclusive illustration of Hardy's understanding and appreciation of drinking matters: 'It was of the most beautiful colour that the eye of an artist in beer could desire; full in body, yet brisk as a volcano; piquant, yet without a twang; luminous as an autumn sunset; free from streakiness of taste, but finally, rather heady'. No wine buff could come up with a more lusciously evocative description.

Pete Bunten has written a novel, a range of magazine articles and some award-winning plays. He arrived by accident in Chesterfield and has yet to find a reason to leave

Roger Buck is a graphic artist. He lives in Chesterfield, conveniently close to several excellent public houses, but prefers bars where, as Tom Waits says ...."*no one speaks English and everything's broken*"